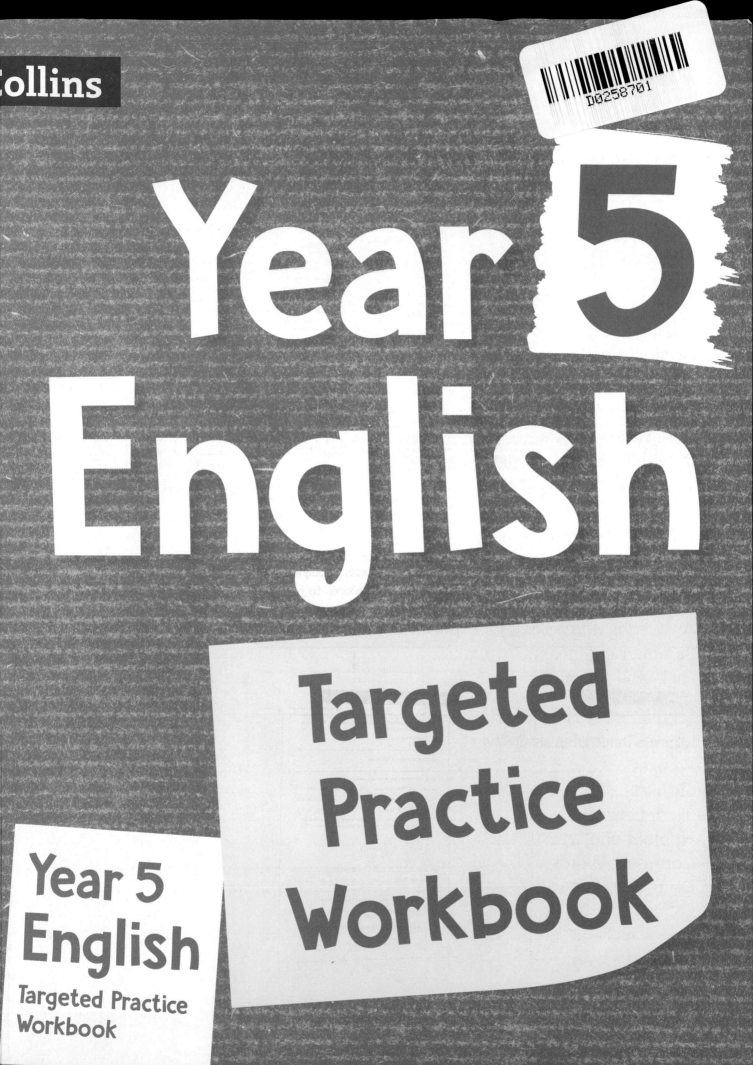

Collins

Year 5 English

Targeted Practice Workbook

Year 5 English
Targeted Practice Workbook

Rachel Axten-Higgs

Contents

Contents

P **1** Rewrite these sentences, putting in the correct punctuation.

    a) the children met at the entrance to the zoo

    <u>The children met at the entrance to the zoo.</u>

    b) have you lost your car keys

    <u>Have you lost your car keys?</u>

    c) what big ears you have grandma

    <u>What big ears you have grandma!</u>

    d) i need to catch the bus home

    <u>I need to catch the bushome.</u>

4 marks

P **2.** Tick the correctly punctuated sentence.

    a) "Please can you help me asked Peter?" ☐

    b) "Please can you help me?" asked Peter. ☑

    c) "Please can you help me," asked Peter. ☐

    d) "Please can you help me" asked Peter. ☐

1 mark

S **3.** Write the plurals for each of these words.

    a) lion   <u>lions</u> ✓

    b) fox   <u>foxes</u> ✓

    c) snail   <u>snails</u>✓

    d) zoo   <u>zoo's</u> ✓

    e) hero   <u>heroes</u> ✓

    f) half   <u>~~halfs~~ halves</u> ✓

    g) baby   <u>babbies</u> ✓

    h) sheep   <u>sheep</u> ✓

8 marks

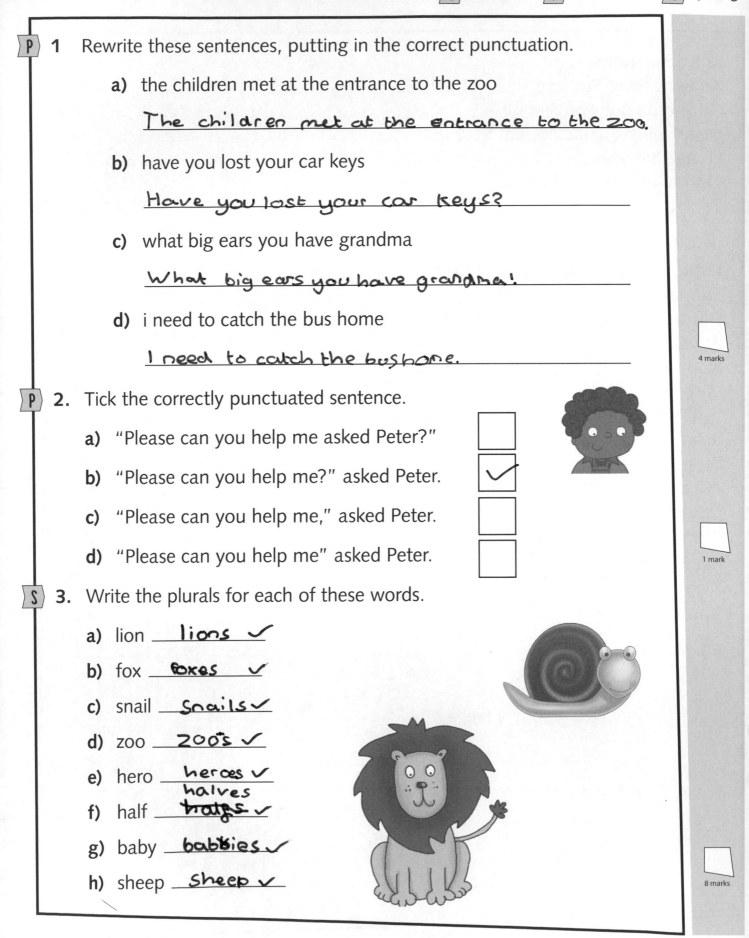

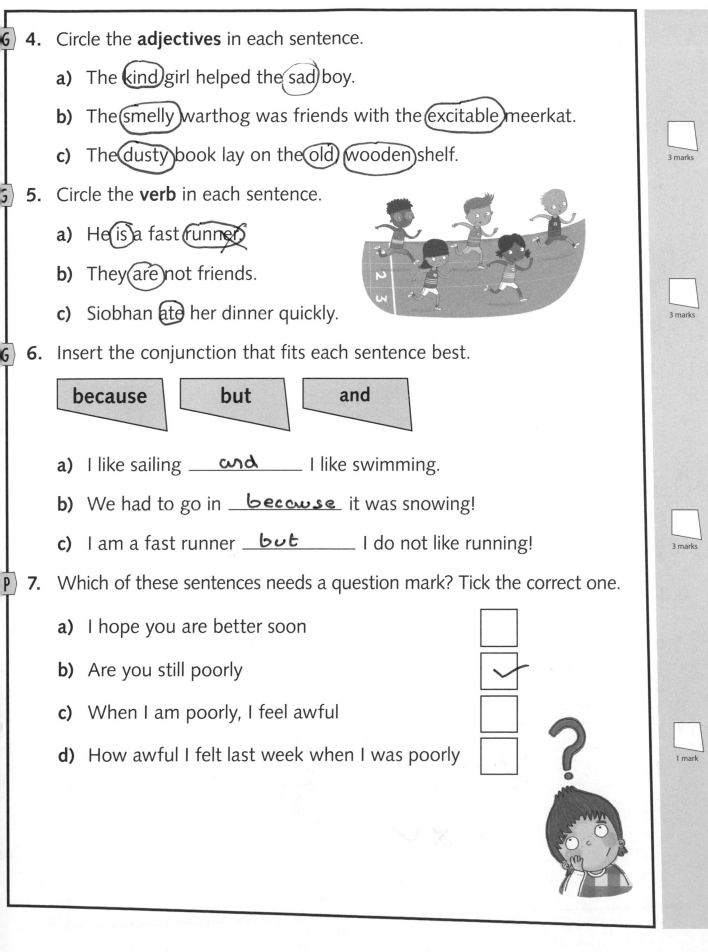

4. Circle the **adjectives** in each sentence.

a) The (kind) girl helped the (sad) boy.

b) The (smelly) warthog was friends with the (excitable) meerkat.

c) The (dusty) book lay on the (old) (wooden) shelf.

3 marks

5. Circle the **verb** in each sentence.

a) He (is) a fast (runner.)

b) They (are) not friends.

c) Siobhan (ate) her dinner quickly.

3 marks

6. Insert the conjunction that fits each sentence best.

| because | but | and |

a) I like sailing ___*and*___ I like swimming.

b) We had to go in ___*because*___ it was snowing!

c) I am a fast runner ___*but*___ I do not like running!

3 marks

7. Which of these sentences needs a question mark? Tick the correct one.

a) I hope you are better soon ☐

b) Are you still poorly ✓

c) When I am poorly, I feel awful ☐

d) How awful I felt last week when I was poorly ☐

1 mark

5

P **8.** Circle the words that should begin with a capital letter.

sebastian ✓   christmas ✓   television   germany ✓

reference   june ✓   monday ✓   newspaper

5 marks

P **9.** Put a comma in the correct place in this sentence.

Before we left,the children checked their luggage.

1 mark

P **10.** Which of these sentences needs an exclamation mark? Tick the correct one.

a) What a strange day it has been ☐ ✓

b) What did you have for dinner ☐

c) Mars is a planet in our solar system ✓ ✗

d) James has a pet dog ☐

1 mark

G **11.** Write each verb in the simple past tense.

a) help _____helped ✓_____

b) fly _____Flyed ✗ flew_____

c) give _____gave ✗ ✓_____

3 marks

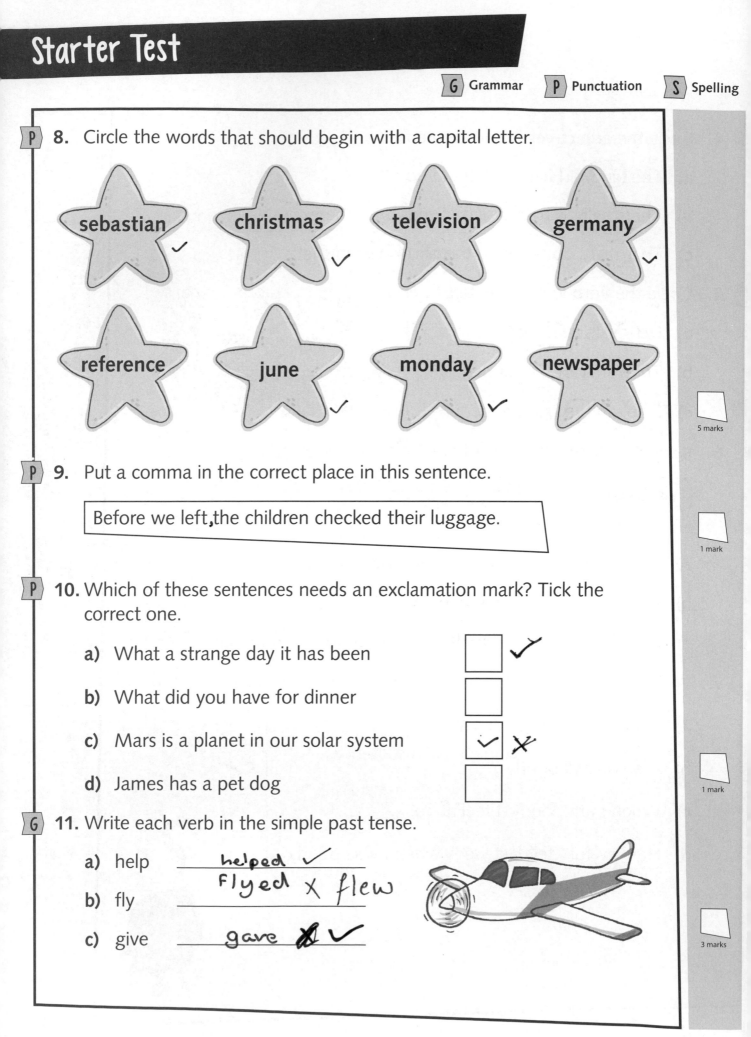

12. Add a prefix to each of these words.

   a) __re__ cycle   b) __un__ fair   c) __dis__ obey

3 marks

13. Add a suffix to each word that has a gap.

   a) He gent __ly__ placed the baby in the cot.

   b) There was a huge amount of excite __ment__ about the party.

   c) Jake is tall __er__ than Owen.

   d) The spring in the launchpad is very power __Full__ .

4 marks

14. Rewrite these sentences putting speech marks in the correct places.

   a) "I am not happy about this," said the teacher.

   _____

   b) Chan whispered, "I am very bored!"

   _____

2 marks

15. Circle the preposition in each sentence.

   a) The children hid (behind) the door.

   b) The pirates climbed (up) the ladder.

   c) Mermaids live (under) the sea.

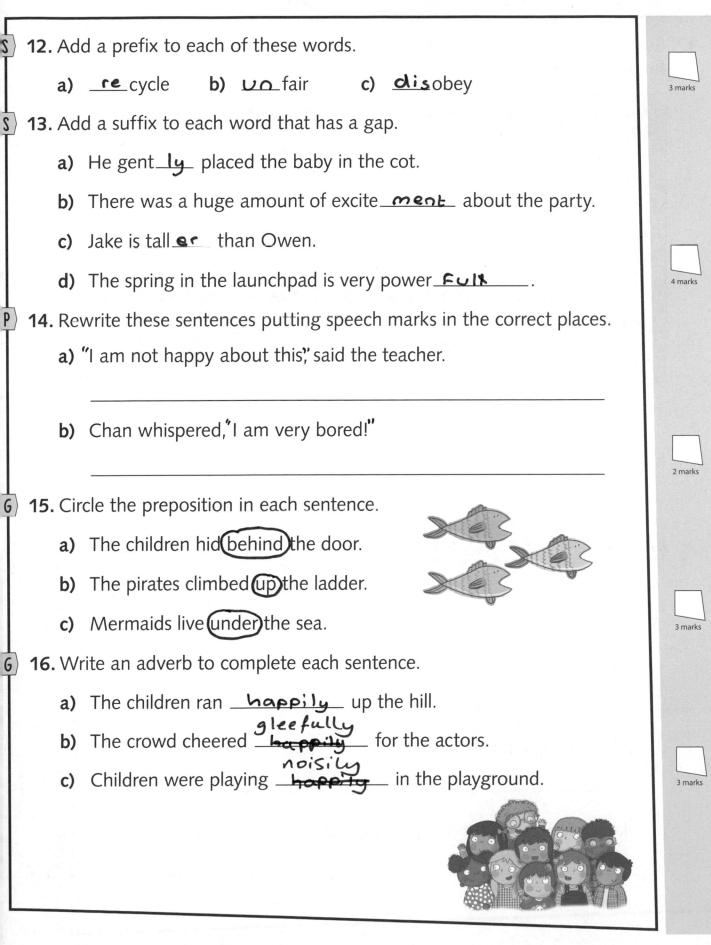

3 marks

16. Write an adverb to complete each sentence.

   a) The children ran __happily__ up the hill.

   b) The crowd cheered __gleefully__ ~~happily~~ for the actors.

   c) Children were playing __noisily__ ~~happily~~ in the playground.

3 marks

7

17. Read the passage and answer the questions. Answer in full sentences.

> Frogs are amazing creatures. There are more than 5,000 different species of frog in the world. They are amphibians, which means they can breathe underwater and on land. Most frogs start their lives as frogspawn (the eggs laid by the adult female), which then develop into tadpoles and then into frogs. A very few are born as full frogs, which means they can be born and live far away from water.
>
> Their main diet is insects and small animals (like earthworms, minnows and spiders). A very interesting fact about frogs is that they do not need to drink water as they are able to absorb it through their skin.

a) How many species of frog are there in the world? _____

_____

b) How do most frogs start their lives? _____

_____

c) What can the frogs that are born as 'full frogs' do?

_____

_____

d) Why do frogs not need to drink water? _____

_____

e) Name two small animals that frogs eat. _____

_____

5 marks

18. The letters in these words are jumbled up. Write the words correctly.

a) deidce   _____

b) tpoisnoi   _____

c) etonci   _____

d) ftuir   _____

e) pgruo   _____

f) gdrau   _____

g) dbiul   _____

h) rrevia   _____

8 marks

19. Write the following words in their contracted form.

a) do not   _____

b) can not   _____

c) will not _____

d) I will   _____

4 marks

20. Write either **a** or **an** before the following words.

a) _____ cup

b) _____ elephant

c) _____ alien

d) _____ phone

e) _____ friend

f) _____ yacht

6 marks

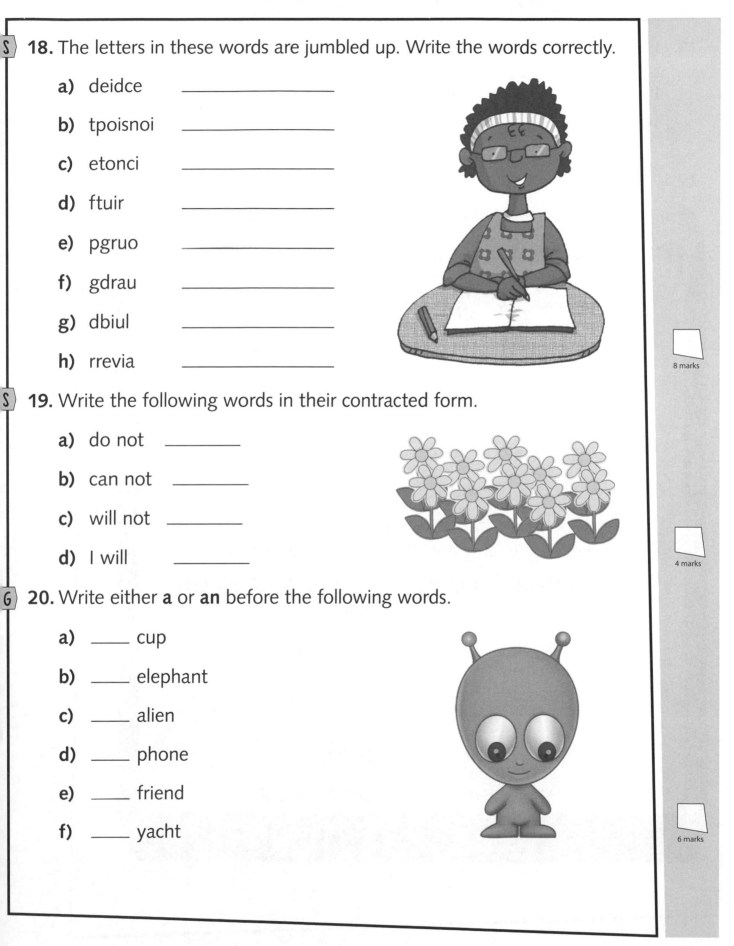

G Grammar   P Punctuation   S Spelling

G **21.** Underline the subordinate clause in this sentence.

Before he could leave the house, James had to unlock the <u>front door</u>.

1 mark

22. Read the advert and answer the questions.

ROBOT X953-7

Do you need more help with your school work?

Would you like more free time?

Help is on hand! Robot X953-7 has whizzed onto the market as a leading home tutor! It is truly amazing!

WHY BOTHER TO DO THE WORK YOURSELF WHEN X953-7 CAN DO IT FOR YOU?

The robot can be named by you and programmed to do your maths and English homework for you. It can even read a book and summarise it for you so you don't have to read it!

BUY IT NOW £79.99!

AVAILABLE IN ALL GOOD TOY SHOPS.

a) What does this advertise?

A robot

b) What does the advert claim it can do?

It can do shool work

c) How could this item save you time with reading?

It can sumarise it for you

d) Write one fact about the thing advertised here.

It can be named by you

e) Write one opinion from the advert.

It is truly amazing!

5 marks

23. Read these sentences. What genre is each sentence? Choose from the options below.

description   persuasion   report

a) Join us this Sunday for fun and frolics on the farm!

persuasion

b) There are many species of penguin in the world.

report

c) It was a white-washed cottage in the middle of a small glade. The roof was thatched and the garden was beautifully kept.

description

3 marks

Marks........ /80

Root Words

G Grammar   **P** Punctuation   **S** Spelling

Challenge 1

S **1** Each set of words has a common root word. Write the root word used in each of these lists.

Example: takes, taken, mistaken   <u>take</u>

a) testing, tested, retest   <u>test</u>

b) tried, untried, trying   <u>try</u>

c) unlikely, dislike, liking   <u>like</u>

d) caring, careless, careful   <u>care</u>

e) unreliable, reliable, relying   <u>rely</u>

5 marks

Marks.......... /5

Challenge 2

A compound word is made when two root words are put together to make a new word.

S **1** Draw a line to match each root word in the first column to one in the second column to make five compound words. Then write each new word.

Root Word	Root Word	New Word
foot	chair	arm chair
light	ball	foot ball
arm	bow	rainbow
pan	house	lighthouse
rain	cake	pancake

5 marks

Marks.......... /5

Root Words

Challenge 3

1 Complete the table below to give two examples of words made from each root word shown.

Root Word	Example 1	Example 2
a) assist	assistance	unascisted
b) cover	covered	uncovered
c) light	lightly	~~onlightly~~ lighter
d) port	porter	~~unport~~ import
e) prove	proven	~~unproved~~ improved

10 marks

2 For each root word shown, circle its meaning in the word family given.

Example: root word: <u>aster</u> / <u>astro</u>
word family: asteroid, astrology, astronomy
meaning: **question /(star)/ thought / life**

a) root word: <u>chrono</u>
word family: chronology, synchronise, chronicle
meaning: **good / light /(time)/ place**

b) root word: <u>geo</u>
word family: geology, geography, geographical
meaning: **ocean /(earth)/ soil / travel**

c) root word: <u>vacuo</u>
word family: vacuate, vacant, vacate
meaning: **(empty)/ travel / closed / see**

d) root word: <u>port</u>
word family: portable, transport, export
meaning: **sound / boat /(carry)/ watch**

4 marks

Marks........./14

Total marks ..../24   How am I doing? 😊 😐 😣

13

Prefixes

Challenge 1

SG **1** Put the correct prefix at the beginning of each word below to create a new word with a different meaning.

| un | dis | mis | pre | sub |

a) _mis_ take

b) _sub_ marine

c) _pre_ view

d) _dis_ respect

e) _un_ hurt

5 marks

2 Draw a line to match each prefix to its meaning.

a) not — sub
b) wrongly — re
c) again — dis
d) before — mis
e) below — pre

5 marks

Marks......... /10

Challenge 2

G **1** Choose the correct root to add to the prefixes shown to complete each sentence below.

| heat | cover | merge | appear |

a) The magician made the rabbit dis _appear_ .

b) They had to un _cover_ the truth.

c) The recipe said to pre _heat_ the oven at the start.

d) They had to sub _merge_ the object in water.

4 marks

Marks......... /4

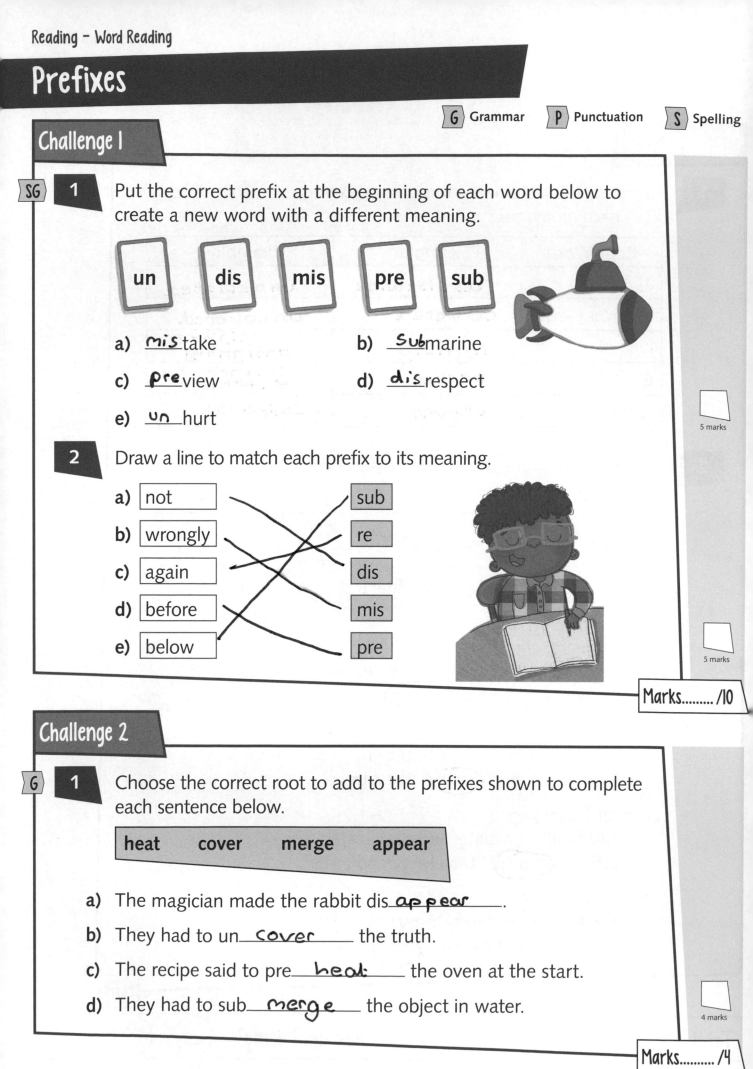

Prefixes

Challenge 3

1 Circle the correct prefix for each word.

a) pre / (un) / mis comfortable

b) (re) / pro / dis written

c) (pre) / re / sub caution

d) (re) / un / mis turn

e) (un) / dis / sub tied

f) re / (mis) / un behave

g) pre / (re) / dis do

7 marks

2 Put the correct prefix in front of each word. Use each prefix only once. Then draw a line to match each new word with its meaning.

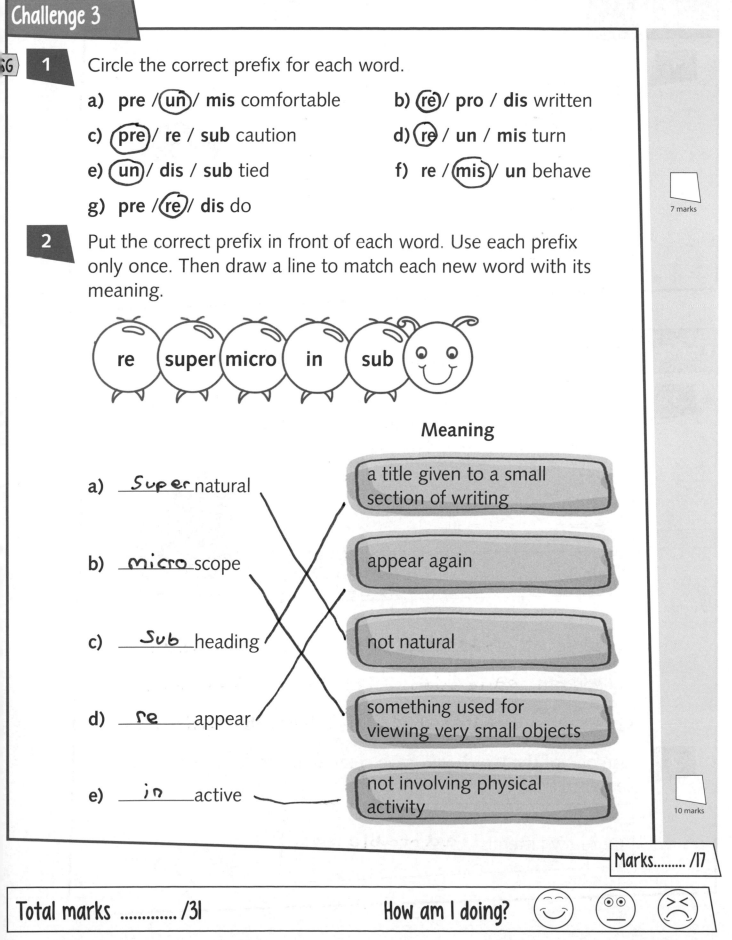

Meaning

a) _Super_ natural

b) _micro_ scope

c) _Sub_ heading

d) _re_ appear

e) _in_ active

a title given to a small section of writing

appear again

not natural

something used for viewing very small objects

not involving physical activity

10 marks

Marks......... /17

Total marks .... /31

How am I doing?

15

Suffixes

G Grammar   P Punctuation   S Spelling

Challenge 1

S | **1**   Circle the suffix at the end of the words below. Think carefully about which part of the word forms the suffix.

a) proud(est)

b) child(ish)

c) glad(ly)

d) care(ful)

e) cold(er)

f) help(less)

g) excite(ment)

h) kind(ness)

8 marks

Marks.......... /8

Challenge 2

S | **1**   Use one of the suffixes below to make a new word from each of those given below. You may need to change the spelling of the root word before adding the suffix.

-tion   -able

Example: frustrate   frustra*tion*

a) adore   _adorable_

b) vacate _vacation_

c) educate _education_

d) desire _desirable_

e) agree   _agreeable_

f) attract _attraction_

6 marks

2   Use one of the words you have created above to complete this sentence:

Our new kitten is _adorable_.

1 mark

Marks......... /7

Suffixes

Challenge 3

1 Use the words ending with a suffix in the box to correctly complete each sentence.

> explanation   thoughtful   hopeless   celebration
> greatest   sadly   warmer   greatness

a) The situation was ___hopeless___ as the car was stuck in the sand.

b) The football team held a ___celebration___ when they won the cup final.

c) The child was ___thoughtful___ as he stared at the page of questions.

d) When she won the competition it was the ___greatest___ day of her life!

e) ___Sadly___, some animals are becoming extinct.

f) He gave an ___explanation___ of what he had found out from his research.

g) Superman liked to show off his ___greatness___ whenever he had the chance!

h) It is usually ___warmer___ in Spain that it is in England.

8 marks

2 Complete these sentences by adding a suitable word ending with a suffix.

a) I ___slowly___ walked to school.

b) It was the ___greatest___ day of my week.

c) He was ___sitting___ on a chair.

d) The child was ___thinking___ what to do next.

4 marks

Marks.........../12

Total marks .... /27   How am I doing?   😊   😐   😣

Adding Prefixes and Suffixes to Root Words

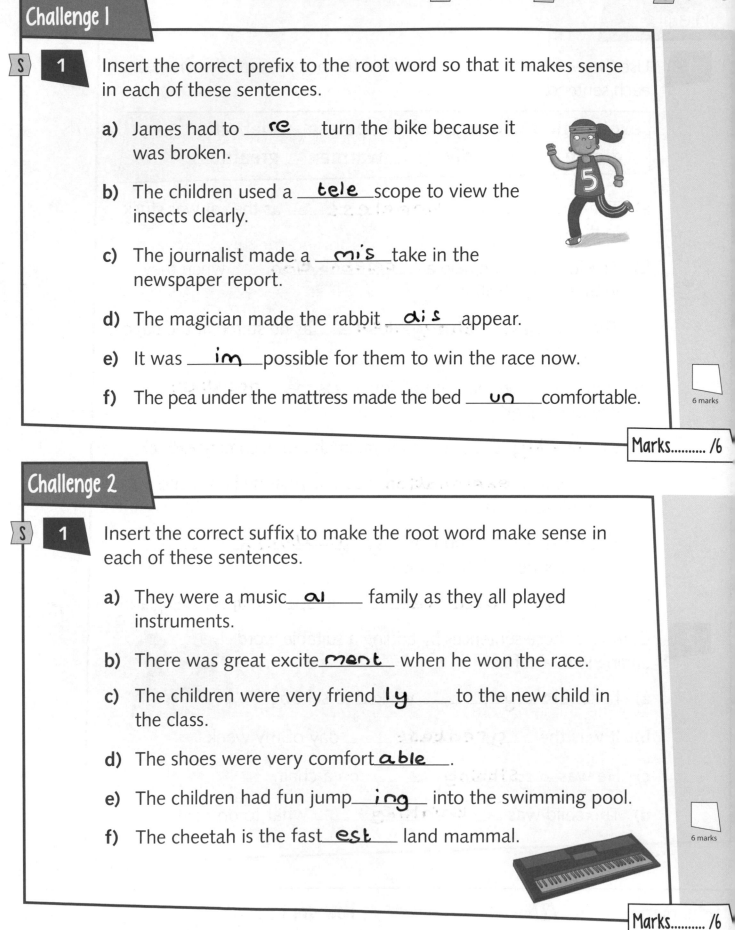

G Grammar   P Punctuation   S Spelling

Challenge 1

S **1**   Insert the correct prefix to the root word so that it makes sense in each of these sentences.

a) James had to ___re___turn the bike because it was broken.

b) The children used a ___tele___scope to view the insects clearly.

c) The journalist made a ___mis___take in the newspaper report.

d) The magician made the rabbit ___dis___appear.

e) It was ___im___possible for them to win the race now.

f) The pea under the mattress made the bed ___un___comfortable.

6 marks

Marks.......... /6

Challenge 2

S **1**   Insert the correct suffix to make the root word make sense in each of these sentences.

a) They were a music___al___ family as they all played instruments.

b) There was great excite___ment___ when he won the race.

c) The children were very friend___ly___ to the new child in the class.

d) The shoes were very comfort___able___.

e) The children had fun jump___ing___ into the swimming pool.

f) The cheetah is the fast___est___ land mammal.

6 marks

Marks.......... /6

Adding Prefixes and Suffixes to Root Words

Challenge 3

1 Add one of the suffixes in the box to the root word to make a new word so that the sentence makes sense. You can use any suffix more than once. Remember, you may need to change the spelling of the root word before adding the suffix.

| ing | ed | ful | ence | er | est | ly | ible | able |

a) They used a refer_**ence**_ book to find the answer to their question.

b) He prefer_**ed**_ to eat jam rather than marmite on his toast.

c) There was a lot of cough_**ing**_ in assembly this morning!

d) The band merry_**ily**_ played their tunes.

e) I am happy_**er**_ in the summer than in the winter!

f) It was the sad_**est**_ I had ever felt.

g) The radio was port_**able**_ so I took it into the garden.

h) The monkeys cheeky_**ly**_ stole the man's hat!

i) I had to be very sense_**able**_ when I crossed the road.

9 marks

2 Write your own word containing a suffix or a prefix to each sentence.

a) The children were ___**determined**___ to find treasure at the end of the rainbow.

b) We had a very ___~~everlasting~~ **uncomfortable**___ night because it was so hot.

2 marks

Marks.......... /11

Total marks .... /23   How am I doing?   😊   😐   😣

19

Homophones and Confusing Words

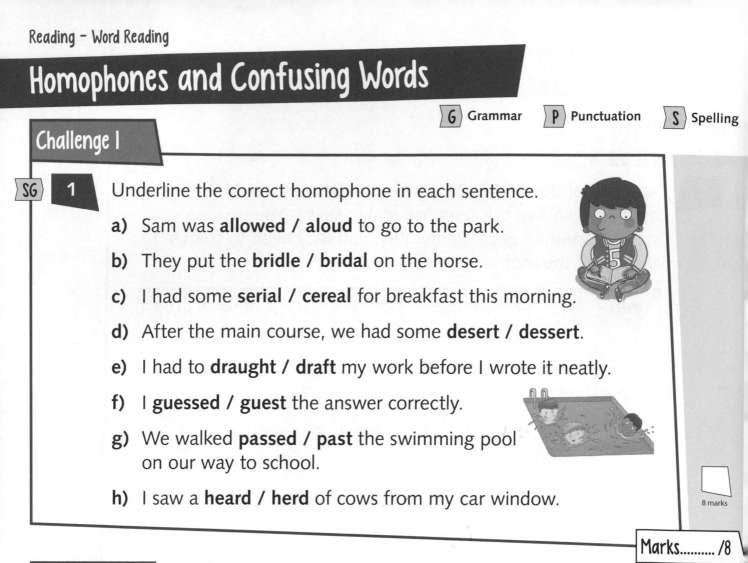

G Grammar   P Punctuation   S Spelling

Challenge 1

SG **1** Underline the correct homophone in each sentence.

a) Sam was **allowed / aloud** to go to the park.

b) They put the **bridle / bridal** on the horse.

c) I had some **serial / cereal** for breakfast this morning.

d) After the main course, we had some **desert / dessert**.

e) I had to **draught / draft** my work before I wrote it neatly.

f) I **guessed / guest** the answer correctly.

g) We walked **passed / past** the swimming pool on our way to school.

h) I saw a **heard / herd** of cows from my car window.

8 marks

Marks.......... /8

Challenge 2

SG **1** Write the correct homophone in the gap in each sentence.

a) **knight / night**   The _____ rode bravely on his horse.

b) **led / lead**   The man _____ the horse along the beach.

c) **farther / father**   Her _____ picked her up from school.

d) **dissent / descent**   They made their _____ down the mountain.

e) **advice / advise**   The teacher gave the child a good piece of _____.

5 marks

Homophones and Confusing Words

2 Write a sentence that contains each of the following words.

a) isle _____

_____

b) aisle _____

_____

2 marks

Marks.......... /7

Challenge 3

1 In each sentence, underline the homophone(s) used incorrectly. Then write the correct homophone(s) above the underlined word(s).

a) The be flew out of his hive.

b) The which flew across the sky on her broomstick.

c) They had to clean the flaw after they spilt the milk.

d) They court the biggest fish they had ever scene.

e) The most important guessed at the wedding was her farther.

f) The banned were aloud to play their music in the mourning.

10 marks

2 Circle the correct choice of word to make each sentence make sense.

a) She bought a new mobile **devise / device** with her pocket money.

b) They went to netball **practice / practise** after school.

c) "**Who's / Whose** been eating my porridge?"

3 marks

Marks......... /13

Total marks .... /28

How am I doing? 😊 😐 😣

Synonyms and Antonyms

G Grammar   P Punctuation   S Spelling

Challenge 1

S **1** Draw a line to link each word with its synonym.

super	hard
difficult	amble
happy	fantastic
kind	large
walk	joyful
big	caring

6 marks

Marks.......... /6

Challenge 2

S **1** Write the antonym to each word shown. Use each word in the box only once.

cold   under   noisy   correct   after   far

a) quiet _____   b) over _____

c) near _____   d) before _____

e) wrong _____   f) hot _____

6 marks

2 Read each sentence and write the antonym of each word underlined.

a) They washed in <u>clean</u> water.   _____

b) They could hear a <u>loud</u> noise in the house. _____

c) The test was very <u>difficult</u>.   _____

3 marks

Marks.......... /9

Synonyms and Antonyms

Challenge 3

1 Replace the words underlined in these sentences with a synonym from the words below so that each sentence makes sense.

alike   man   close   wrong   over

a) The school day was <u>finished</u>.   _____

b) The young <u>chap</u> looked smart in his suit.   _____

c) Most of the answers were <u>incorrect</u>.   _____

d) They all looked <u>similar</u> in their school uniform.   _____

e) The shop was very <u>near</u> to their house.   _____

5 marks

2 Complete the table to show the synonym and antonym for each word. The first line has been done for you.

Word	Synonym	Antonym
pretty	*beautiful*	*ugly*
rich		
young		
expensive		
stop		

10 marks

Marks......... /15

Total marks .... /30   How am I doing?   😊   😐   😣

23

Text Types

Challenge 1

1 Read the text and answer the questions below.

Family Fun at the Farm

Home Farm is flinging open its doors to welcome you and your family to experience the hidden wonders it has to offer. For one day only (Sunday 16th July) you can come and enjoy our wonderful facilities. There will be tractor demonstrations, sheep-shearing, tractor rides, musical entertainment and much more. Open 10 am – 4 pm, you can enjoy the whole day with us, drinking homemade apple juice and eating burgers, prize-winning sausages and more from our barbecue! Come and enjoy the fun!

a) What genre is the text? _____

1 mark

b) How long is the farm open for? _____

1 mark

c) Write down two things you can do. _____

_____

2 marks

d) What is the purpose of the text? _____

1 mark

Marks.......... /5

Challenge 2

1 Read these sentences. What genre are they? Choose from the words in the box.

description	persuasion	recount

a) We had a great day at the zoo.
First we went to see the monkeys. _____

b) The view was amazing, the rolling green fields and small defining hedges made it look like the perfect English countryside. _____

c) FastRun – the only trainers if you need to succeed. Try them, buy them, love them. _____

3 marks

Marks.......... /3

Text Types

1 Read each extract and circle the genre it comes from.

a)

> **Shark Attacks Surfer**
> An Australian surfer had a very lucky escape yesterday when the board he was paddling on was attacked by a shark. The surfer managed to hit the shark on the nose with the board and swim swiftly to shore.

diary / instructions / biography / newspaper / poetry

b)

> What a cool day! Didn't think I would be writing about such an exciting event. Today, I actually managed all the skills I needed for my next trampolining badge. Concentrated really hard and am so proud of myself! Hooray!

diary / instructions / biography / newspaper / poetry

c)

> If I had a paintbrush I would paint…
> A shooting star gliding across the beautiful night sky.

diary / instructions / biography / newspaper / poetry

d)

> Jessica Ennis-Hill was born on 28th January 1986 in Sheffield. She has one sister, called Carmel. Her father is Jamaican and her mother is English…

diary / instructions / biography / newspaper / poetry

4 marks

Marks.........../4

Total marks ..../12   How am I doing?   😊   😐   😣

Structures and Meanings

G Grammar   P Punctuation   S Spelling

Challenge 1

1 Draw a line to join each genre to a typical structural feature you would expect to see in it.

| newspaper | recipe | story | advert |

| beginning, middle and end | slogans | written in columns | numbered steps |

4 marks

Marks.........../4

Challenge 2

1 Read the text and answer the questions below.

There once lived a little old woman and a little old man. One day, the little old woman decided to bake some gingerbread men. She had made them many times before. However, today was going to prove to be very different from the other times she had made them…

As the gingerbread men were baking, the little old woman sat at the kitchen table and read her magazine until she heard a noise. It was not a loud noise but it was definitely an unusual noise. It seemed to come from the oven. When she walked over to the oven she saw one of the gingerbread men knocking on the oven door. Knocking?

a) Find and write the sentence that shows it was not the first time the little old woman had baked gingerbread men.

_____

_____

1 mark

b) Find and write the sentence that the author has used to show us that something strange is going to happen in the story.

_____

_____

1 mark

Structures and Meanings

c) Write down two things we are told about the noise that is heard.

_____

2 marks

Marks.......... /4

Challenge 3

1 Read the text and answer the questions.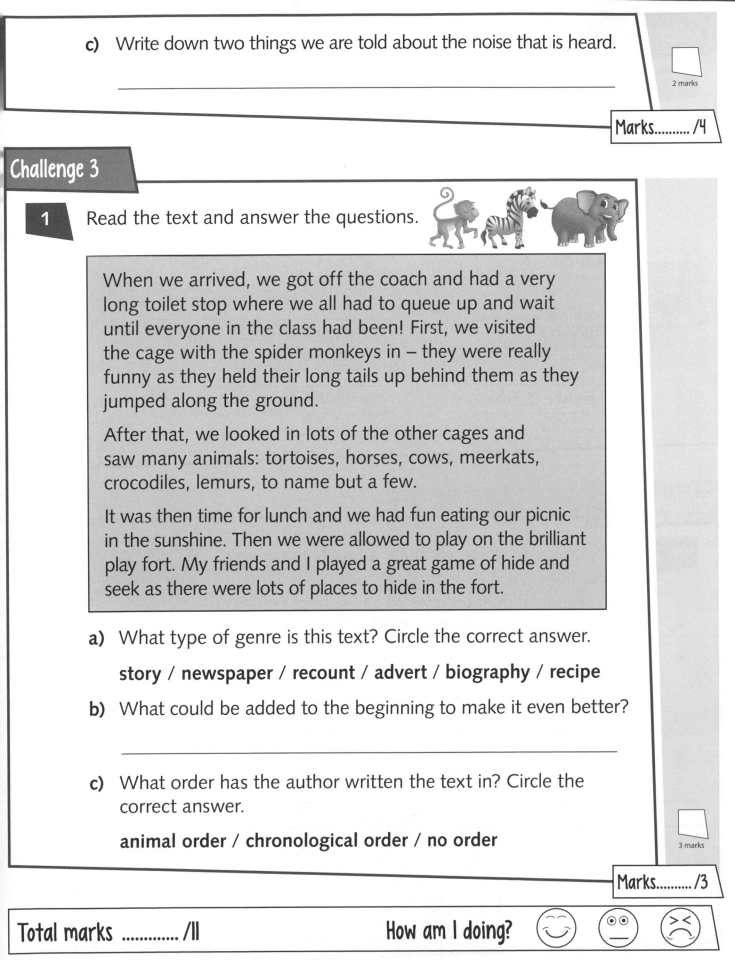

> When we arrived, we got off the coach and had a very long toilet stop where we all had to queue up and wait until everyone in the class had been! First, we visited the cage with the spider monkeys in – they were really funny as they held their long tails up behind them as they jumped along the ground.
>
> After that, we looked in lots of the other cages and saw many animals: tortoises, horses, cows, meerkats, crocodiles, lemurs, to name but a few.
>
> It was then time for lunch and we had fun eating our picnic in the sunshine. Then we were allowed to play on the brilliant play fort. My friends and I played a great game of hide and seek as there were lots of places to hide in the fort.

a) What type of genre is this text? Circle the correct answer.

story / newspaper / recount / advert / biography / recipe

b) What could be added to the beginning to make it even better?

_____

c) What order has the author written the text in? Circle the correct answer.

animal order / chronological order / no order

3 marks

Marks.......... /3

Total marks .... /11   How am I doing?   😊   😐   😣

Themes and Conventions

G Grammar   P Punctuation   S Spelling

Challenge 1

1 Draw a line to match each story genre to its definition.

fantasy	the characters go somewhere exciting / dangerous / fun
myth	ideas including space, time travel and the future
adventure	a traditional story involving supernatural beings and / or events
mystery	imagined places and people – not based in reality
science fiction	something has to be solved

5 marks

Marks.......... /5

Challenge 2

1 For each genre, there are quite a few features and conventions, such as typical settings used. Write each setting shown below into the correct column of the table to show which genre it is **most likely** to be linked to.

police station   magical castle   little cottage   planets

moon   spaceships   jewellery shop   forest

Mystery	Fairy Tale	Science Fiction

8 marks

Marks.......... /8

Themes and Conventions

Challenge 3

1 Read each extract and circle the genre that it fits best into.

a)

> Hermes (the winged messenger of the gods) flew down to talk to Hades. He wanted to ask what the matter was as he was clearly unhappy about something. Before Hermes could ask, Hades swept Persephone (Demeter's daughter) into his chariot and rode away with her back down to the underworld…

myth / fantasy / adventure / mystery / horror / science fiction

b)

> "So what has been stolen?" asked DCI Locke. His eyes swept the untidy room; someone had obviously been searching for something. "It's Mrs Bennett's pearl necklace, Sir," replied DS James…

myth / fantasy / adventure / mystery / horror / science fiction

c)

> Jamel pushed opened the creaky door. He held his breath. Music could be heard, strange eerie music. His heart raced and sweat poured from his brow. He pushed the door open further, something flew out. He screamed and ran…

myth / fantasy / adventure / mystery / horror / science fiction

d)

> There were lasers coming from all sides. Chris froze. What could he do? He concentrated hard and looked at the control panel. What if he pressed the green button…? He breathed in rapidly and pressed it. Suddenly he was moving through space at what could only be the speed of light. He had left his enemies behind…

myth / fantasy / adventure / mystery / horror / science fiction

e)

> It was windier, much windier than we had expected as we reached the summit. Each step was an effort as the wind tried to push us backwards. It was cold too, the higher we went, the colder it had got. What an amazing finale to all our planning and preparations…

myth / fantasy / adventure / mystery / horror / science fiction

5 marks

Marks.......... /5

Total marks .... /18   How am I doing? 😊 😐 😣

Comparing Texts

G Grammar   P Punctuation   S Spelling

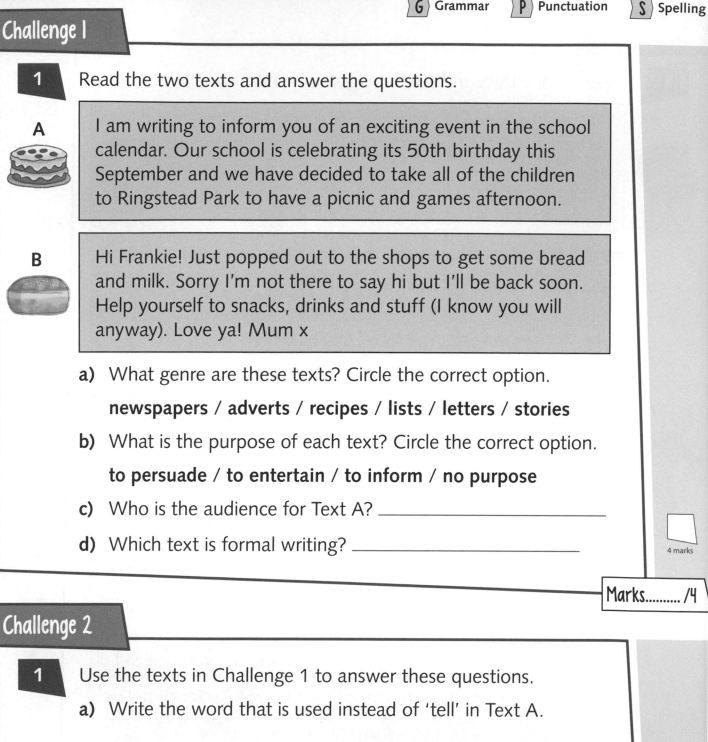

1 Read the two texts and answer the questions.

A

I am writing to inform you of an exciting event in the school calendar. Our school is celebrating its 50th birthday this September and we have decided to take all of the children to Ringstead Park to have a picnic and games afternoon.

B

Hi Frankie! Just popped out to the shops to get some bread and milk. Sorry I'm not there to say hi but I'll be back soon. Help yourself to snacks, drinks and stuff (I know you will anyway). Love ya! Mum x

a) What genre are these texts? Circle the correct option.

newspapers / adverts / recipes / lists / letters / stories

b) What is the purpose of each text? Circle the correct option.

to persuade / to entertain / to inform / no purpose

c) Who is the audience for Text A? _____

d) Which text is formal writing? _____

4 marks

Marks.......... /4

Challenge 2

1 Use the texts in Challenge 1 to answer these questions.

a) Write the word that is used instead of 'tell' in Text A.

_____

b) Write the word that is used instead of 'gone' in Text B.

_____

c) What does the part in brackets in Text B tell us about Frankie?

_____

_____

3 marks

Marks.......... /3

Comparing Texts

Challenge 3

1 Read the two texts and answer the questions.

A

Dear Diary. As always, I worked hard on the farm today. I had to help my father to feed all of the animals and make sure they had water to drink. This took a long  time but was very rewarding work as the animals know me now and come near as if to say "hello". After my luncheon of mutton, bread and water, I had to do the worst job of all: clean out the Shire horses.

B

Dear Diary. Today was awesome – firstly it was my birthday! I'M NOW 10 YEARS OLD! Even school was fun as it was sports day so we didn't have many lessons! I won the sprint race too so got a shiny gold medal! After school, Mum took me and my mates to the skatepark and we had great fun. After that we ate burgers for dinner. The perfect day!

a) Look at the style of each text. Which diary is **not** written by a modern child? _____

b) Explain your answer to part **a)**.

_____

c) Write a word from Text B that would not appear in formal writing. _____

d) Which day would you have most liked to have? _____

e) Explain your answer.

_____

5 marks

Marks.........../5

Total marks .... /12   How am I doing?   ☺ 😐 ☹

Types of Poetry

Challenge 1

G **1** Read this poem in your head. Read it aloud to a friend. Learn it by heart and perform it to a group or the class. Try to get the humour of the poem across.

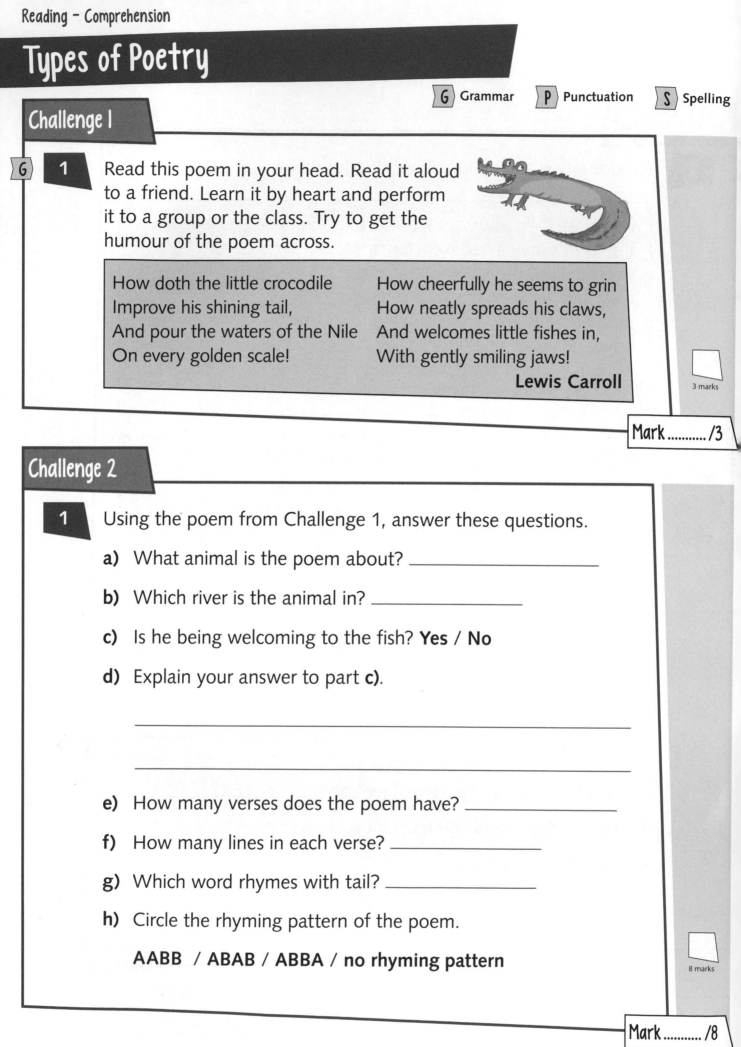

> How doth the little crocodile   How cheerfully he seems to grin
> Improve his shining tail,   How neatly spreads his claws,
> And pour the waters of the Nile   And welcomes little fishes in,
> On every golden scale!   With gently smiling jaws!
>
> **Lewis Carroll**

3 marks

Mark .... /3

Challenge 2

1 Using the poem from Challenge 1, answer these questions.

a) What animal is the poem about? _____

b) Which river is the animal in? _____

c) Is he being welcoming to the fish? **Yes / No**

d) Explain your answer to part **c)**.

_____

_____

e) How many verses does the poem have? _____

f) How many lines in each verse? _____

g) Which word rhymes with tail? _____

h) Circle the rhyming pattern of the poem.

AABB / ABAB / ABBA / no rhyming pattern

8 marks

Mark .... /8

Types of Poetry

Challenge 3

1 A syllable is a unit of sound with only one vowel sound. Divide these words into their individual syllables by drawing diagonal lines (/).

Example: s u / p e r

a) d e f i n i t e l y   **b)** h e l p l e s s n e s s

c) e l e p h a n t   **d)** l i s t e n i n g

4 marks

2 A cinquain has five lines and the syllable pattern is 2 / 4 / 6 / 8 / 2. Read this cinquain and draw diagonal lines (/) to show where the syllables are.

Cool breeze,

Sparkling water,

Sun blazing on my back.

Golden sand between my warm toes…

the beach.

5 marks

3 A haiku has three lines. Read this haiku, then divide each line into syllables and work out the syllable count for each.

Green and scaled legs,

Squelching slowly through the mud

Watching for its prey.

3 marks

Marks.........../12

Total marks ..../23   How am I doing?   😊 😐 😣

Playscripts

Challenge 1

1 Match these well-known characters to their actions.

Peter Pan	breaks into a house
Goldilocks	is scared of a mouse
The Gruffalo	blows down houses
Big Bad Wolf	fights a bad pirate

4 marks

Marks.......... /4

Read the playscript below and use it to answer the questions in Challenges 2 and 3.

Scene 1: Preparations

The scene is the hallway of a family home. The family are preparing to go to the airport. A taxi is waiting outside. Suitcases line the hall.

Dad: Isn't this exciting – our first family holiday overseas.

Mum: *(slightly hysterical)* Exciting? Exciting? Well it might be if we *ever* get there!

James: *(playing a game on his phone)* Just relax Mum, we're ready aren't we? The taxi isn't even here yet.

Mum: *(almost shrieking with hands on hips)* Relax? How can I relax when I'm running round after you three and myself?

Phoebe: *(sulkily, whilst texting on her phone)* Well, I packed my hair straighteners and my hair dryer so you didn't do everything for me.

The door-bell rings

Mum: Arrgh! Now the taxi driver is here too and we're not remotely ready *(trips over dog)* Max, just get out of the way!

Dad: *(opening door)* Hello! Welcome to the mad house!

Frank: *(laughing)* I was a little scared to ring the bell after hearing the shouting!

Dad: *(whispering)* Her bark is worse than her bite!

Dad and Frank begin putting things in the car. Their dog is running about excitedly. Frank trips over the dog.

Frank: *(lying on the floor screaming)* ARRGHHH! My foot, I think I've broken it. Stupid dog!

Playscripts

Challenge 2

1 Answer these questions about the playscript.

a) Why is Mum not excited about the holiday?

_____

b) Why is Frank lying on the floor in pain?

_____

c) What does Dad tell Frank about Mum?

_____

d) What is James doing whilst he is waiting?

_____

4 marks

Marks.......... /4

Challenge 3

12 marks

1 Underline all the stage directions in the playscript.

2 Answer the questions using the playscript to help you.

a) What are the two purposes of stage directions? Circle two answers.

To show how a character is speaking	To show what a character is saying
To tell what is happening	To tell the story
To show what the narrator says	

2 marks

b) What punctuation mark is used after the characters' names before the words they say? _____

1 mark

Marks......... /15

Total marks .... /23   How am I doing?   😊   😐   😣

35

Words in Context

G Grammar   P Punctuation   S Spelling

Challenge 1

SG **1** Words can mean different things in different contexts. For each sentence, circle the meaning of the word in red.

a) It was **break** time at school.

separate into pieces	interruption of continuity	a pause during an activity

b) The children had managed to **break** the swing.

separate into pieces	interruption of continuity	a pause during an activity

2 marks

Marks............/2

Challenge 2

G **1** What does the word 'others' refer to in the text below? Tick the correct option.

> Some countries, such as the UK, USA, Australia and France, have red, blue and white in their flags. Others, such as Germany, Spain and Portugal, have different colours.

(Germany) (Spain) (Portugal) (colours) (countries)

(UK) (USA) (Australia) (France)

1 mark

2 a) Write a sentence that uses the word 'talk' as a **verb**.

_____

b) Write a sentence that uses the word 'talk' as a **noun**.

_____

2 marks

Marks.........../3

Words in Context

Challenge 3

1 Read this poem extract and answer the questions about the words used.

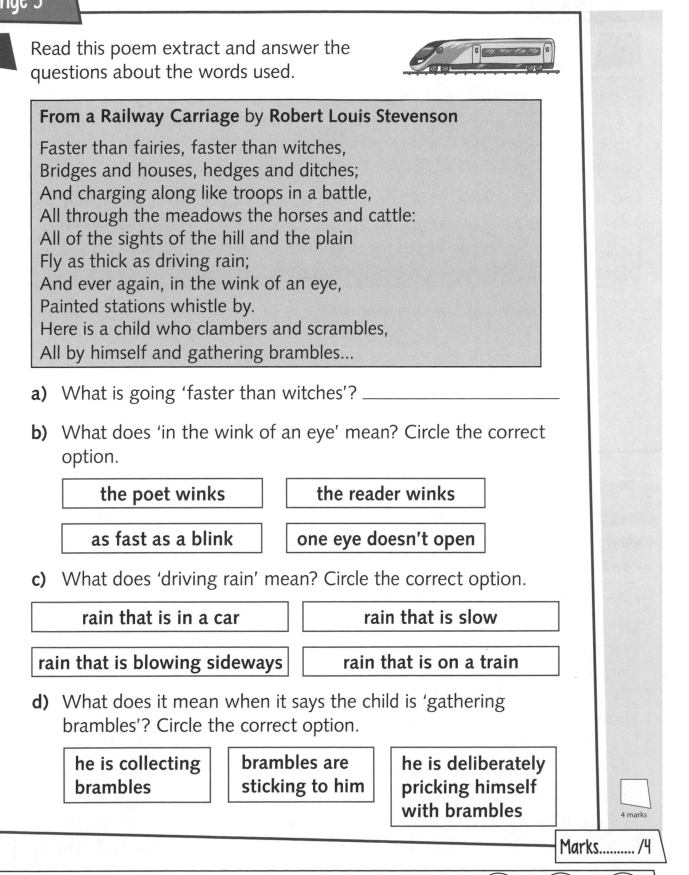

From a Railway Carriage by **Robert Louis Stevenson**

Faster than fairies, faster than witches,
Bridges and houses, hedges and ditches;
And charging along like troops in a battle,
All through the meadows the horses and cattle:
All of the sights of the hill and the plain
Fly as thick as driving rain;
And ever again, in the wink of an eye,
Painted stations whistle by.
Here is a child who clambers and scrambles,
All by himself and gathering brambles...

a) What is going 'faster than witches'? _____

b) What does 'in the wink of an eye' mean? Circle the correct option.

the poet winks	the reader winks
as fast as a blink	one eye doesn't open

c) What does 'driving rain' mean? Circle the correct option.

rain that is in a car	rain that is slow
rain that is blowing sideways	rain that is on a train

d) What does it mean when it says the child is 'gathering brambles'? Circle the correct option.

he is collecting brambles	brambles are sticking to him	he is deliberately pricking himself with brambles

4 marks

Marks.........../4

Total marks ..../9   How am I doing? 😊 😐 😣

37

Drawing Inferences

G Grammar   P Punctuation   S Spelling

Challenge 1

1 Read the text and answer the questions.

> Alice was beginning to get very tired of sitting by her sister on the bank, and of having nothing to do: once or twice she had peeped into the book her sister was reading, but it had no pictures or conversations in it, "and what is the use of a book," thought Alice "without pictures or conversation?"
>
> So she was considering in her own mind (as well as she could, for the hot day made her feel very sleepy and stupid), whether the pleasure of making a daisy-chain would be worth the trouble of getting up and picking the daisies, when suddenly a White Rabbit with pink eyes ran close by her...

a) What was the weather like?

_____

b) What was the problem with making a daisy chain?

_____

2 marks

Marks............/2

Challenge 2

1 Read the text and answer the questions.

> Alice was not a bit hurt, and she jumped up on to her feet in a moment: she looked up, but it was all dark overhead; before her was another long passage, and the White Rabbit was still in sight, hurrying down it. There was not a moment to be lost: away went Alice like the wind, and was just in time to hear it say, as it turned a corner, "Oh my ears and whiskers, how late it's getting!" She was close behind it when she turned the corner, but the Rabbit was no longer to be seen: she found herself in a long, low hall, which was lit up by a row of lamps hanging from the roof.
>
> There were doors all round the hall, but they were all locked; and when Alice had been all the way down one side and up the other, trying every door, she walked sadly down the middle, wondering how she was ever to get out again.

Drawing Inferences

a) Why did Alice run so fast?

_____

b) Write the phrase that tells us Alice went fast.

_____

c) As well as feeling sad, how else does
Alice feel at the end of this? _____

3 marks

Marks.......... /3

Challenge 3

1   Read the text and answer the questions.

One green light squinting over Kidd's Creek, which is near the mouth of the pirate river, marked where the brig, the *Jolly Roger,* lay, low in the water; a rakish-looking craft foul to the hull, every beam in her detestable, like ground strewn with mangled feathers. She was the cannibal of the seas, and scarce needed that watchful eye, for she floated immune in the horror of her name.

a) What was 'the cannibal of the seas'? Circle the correct option.

| Wendy | Tinkerbell | the *Jolly Roger* | the night | Kidd's Creek |

b) What does the 'mouth'
mean in this text? _____

c) Does the author want us to think the *Jolly Roger* is a nice
ship?   **Yes / No**

d) Explain your answer (using a quote from the text) to part **c)**.

_____

_____

4 marks

Marks.......... /4

Total marks .... /9   How am I doing?   ☺ ☺ ☹

Answering and Asking Questions

G Grammar   P Punctuation   S Spelling

Challenge 1

1 Write two questions that you would like to ask an astronaut about his/her work.

a) _____

b) _____

2 marks

Marks............/2

Challenge 2

1 Read the text and answer the questions below.

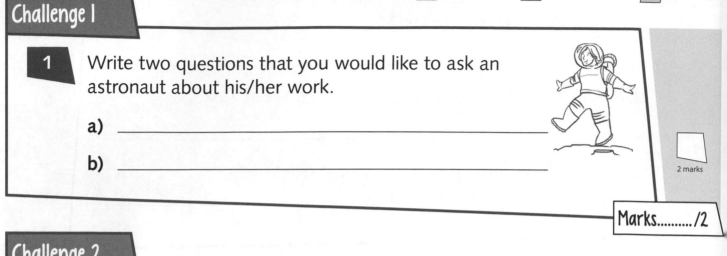

Timothy Peake was born on 7th April 1972. He is a Space Agency Astronaut and has been a member of the International Space Station (ISS). We interviewed him and this is what we found out.

Tim is married and has two sons. He enjoys climbing and caving in his spare time. He likes to keep fit by doing cross-country running and triathlon. He felt honoured to receive a message of support from the Queen after he docked with the International Space Station.

Interview conducted on 8th April 2016

a) How old was Timothy Peake at the time of the interview?

_____

b) Write a question you could ask him about his family that is not answered in the text.

_____

c) What question might have been asked of him that gave the answer about climbing and caving?

_____

3 marks

Marks.........../3

Answering and Asking Questions

Challenge 3

1 Read the text and write a heading on each line in the report. The heading should ask a question that the text answers.

Heading a) _____?

The International Space Station is a large spacecraft that orbits the Earth. It is a home where astronauts live and it also has a science lab. Many countries worked together to build it and therefore they are all able to use it.

Heading b) _____?

The first piece of the International Space Station was launched in 1998. A Russian rocket launched that piece. After that, more pieces were added. Two years later, the station was ready for people. The first crew arrived on 2nd November 2000. There have been people living on the space station ever since.

Heading c) _____?

The Space Station is as big inside as a house with five bedrooms. It has two bathrooms, a gymnasium and a big bay window. It can hold up to six people. It is as big as an American Football pitch.

3 marks

2 Answer these questions about the text above.

a) How many bathrooms does the ISS have? _____

b) When did people start living on the ISS? _____

c) How many people can live on the ISS at one time? _____

d) Why is it called an 'International' Space Station?

_____

4 marks

Marks.........../7

Total marks .... /12   How am I doing? 😊 😐 😣

Summarising Ideas

G Grammar   **P** Punctuation   **S** Spelling

Challenge 1

1   Circle the correct words to complete this definition.

A summary is a **short / long** version of the **draft / original** text. It is usually only a **paragraph / page** long. It picks out the **exciting / main** points only.

4 marks

Marks.......... /4

Challenge 2

1   Read this speech and answer the questions.

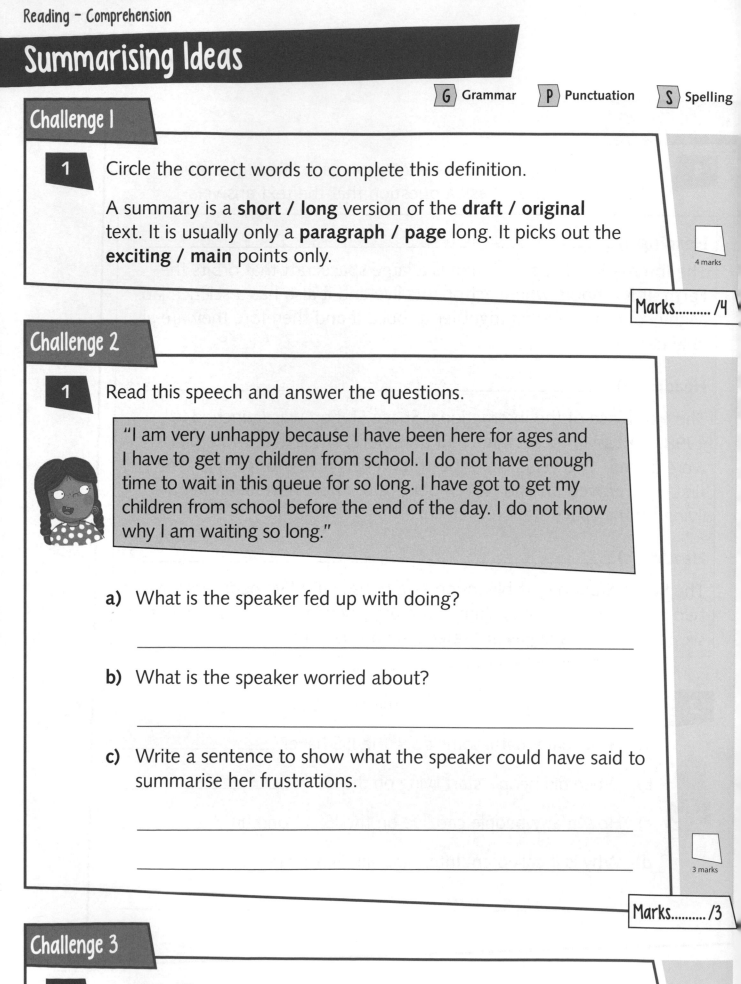

"I am very unhappy because I have been here for ages and I have to get my children from school. I do not have enough time to wait in this queue for so long. I have got to get my children from school before the end of the day. I do not know why I am waiting so long."

a) What is the speaker fed up with doing?

_____

b) What is the speaker worried about?

_____

c) Write a sentence to show what the speaker could have said to summarise her frustrations.

_____

_____

3 marks

Marks.......... /3

Challenge 3

1   Read the letter on the next page and then answer the questions.

Summarising Ideas

Ridgeway Park School
10 Ridgeway Road
Lugworth, LW9 8YT

12 Ridgeway Road,
Lugworth, LW9 8YT

Dear Mrs Clowes,

I am writing to you to express my sincere disappointment at your continued lack of communication with me regarding the parking situation outside YOUR school. I have written to you on numerous occasions and you have still not done anything about it. I am losing my patience. I will have to take it further and contact the Highways Authority.

Yet again there was a coach parked outside the school yesterday morning. It arrived at 8.56 am and did not leave until 8.59 am. It had its engine on the whole time whilst the children were climbing off and walking into school. I am fed up with having to smell the fumes of the coach. Back again it came at 3.12 pm and it didn't leave until 3.20 pm when the children were all on. It is time you acted to put me out of my misery.

Yours sincerely,

Mr A. Noyed

a) Who do you think Mrs Clowes is? Circle the correct answer.

parent / neighbour / Headteacher / cook / Highways Agency worker

b) What is Mr Noyed cross about? Circle two answers.

the school / the fumes / the noise / the size / the children / the driver

c) Is this the first time he has contacted Mrs Clowes about this?
Yes / No

d) Write a phrase that helped you answer part **c)**.

_____

_____

4 marks

Marks.........../4

Total marks .... /11   How am I doing?   ☺ ◉◉ ☹

43

Facts and Opinions

G Grammar   P Punctuation   S Spelling

Challenge 1

1 Circle the correct word to complete each definition.

a) Facts are **false / true** pieces of information.

b) Opinions are based on **personal / true** thoughts and feelings.

2 marks

Marks............/2

Challenge 2

1 Sort these sentences into facts or opinions by writing each letter in the correct column in the table below.

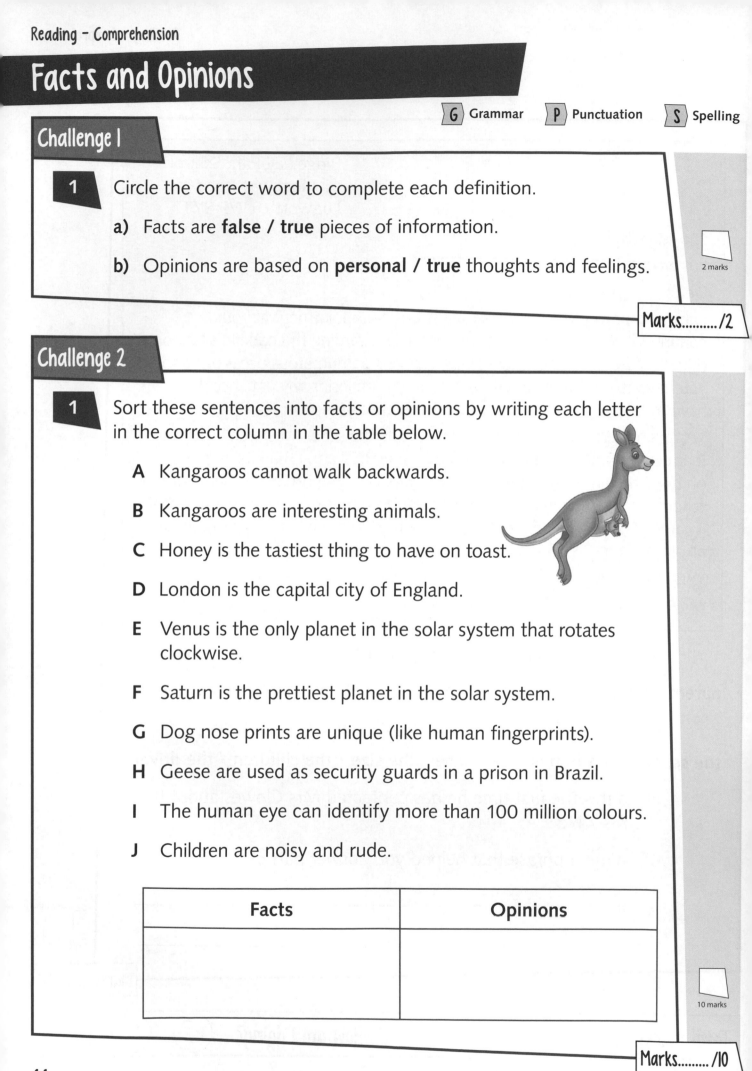

A Kangaroos cannot walk backwards.

B Kangaroos are interesting animals.

C Honey is the tastiest thing to have on toast.

D London is the capital city of England.

E Venus is the only planet in the solar system that rotates clockwise.

F Saturn is the prettiest planet in the solar system.

G Dog nose prints are unique (like human fingerprints).

H Geese are used as security guards in a prison in Brazil.

I The human eye can identify more than 100 million colours.

J Children are noisy and rude.

Facts	Opinions

10 marks

Marks........../10

Facts and Opinions

Challenge 3

1 Read this text. Circle facts and underline opinions.

"This has been the greatest football season ever. Leicester City are the champions! They are also the best team in the world! They will take part in a Victory Parade to show the cup to their supporters. The Premier League trophy is 104 cm high and weighs about 25 kg! I think they might have tired arms after lifting it!"

6 marks

2 **a)** Write a fact about a music group / artist.

_____

b) Write an opinion about the music group / artist in part **a)**.

_____

c) Write a fact about your school.

_____

d) Write an opinion about a sports team.

_____

4 marks

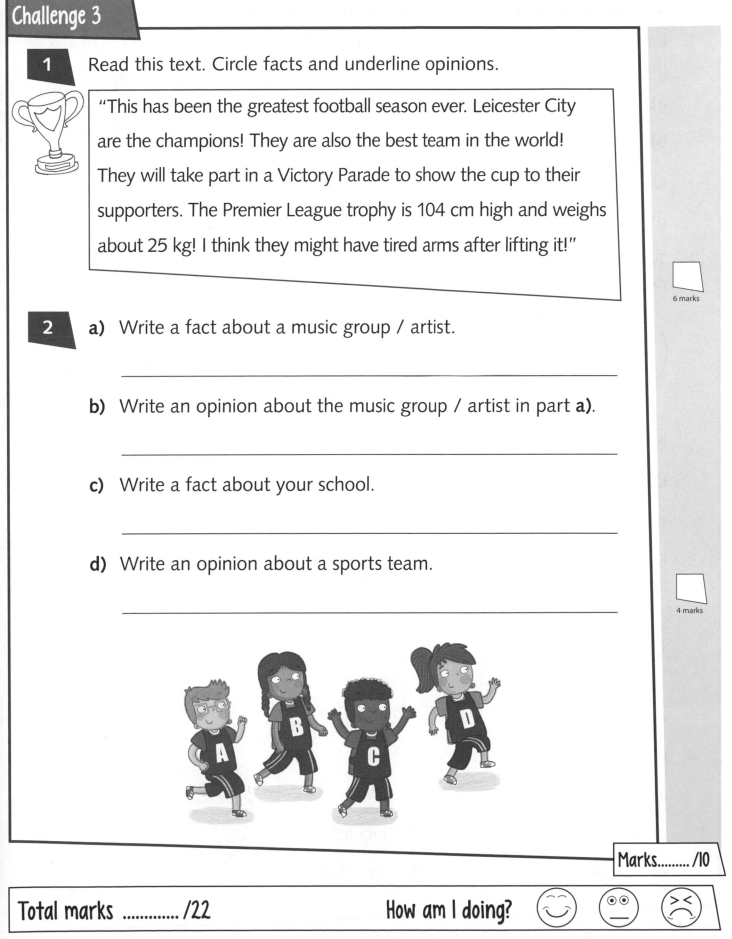

Marks.........../10

Total marks .... /22   How am I doing?   😊   😐   😣

S **1.** Each set of words has a common root word. Write the root word used in each of these lists.

     a) conform, reform, formation _____

     b) transport, portable, report _____

     c) microscope, telescope, periscope _____

     d) supervision, television, revision _____

4 marks

S **2.** Two root words can be put together to make a new word. Write five new words that can be created by putting these root words together.

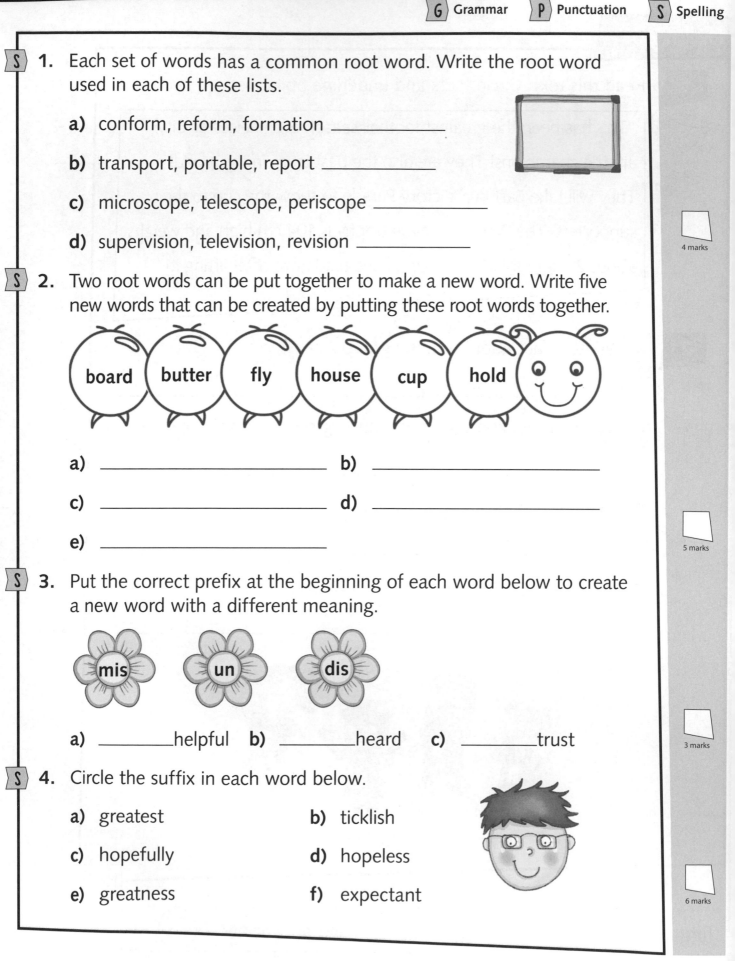

board   butter   fly   house   cup   hold

     a) _____   **b)** _____

     c) _____   **d)** _____

     e) _____

5 marks

S **3.** Put the correct prefix at the beginning of each word below to create a new word with a different meaning.

mis   un   dis

     a) _____helpful   **b)** _____heard   **c)** _____trust

3 marks

S **4.** Circle the suffix in each word below.

     a) greatest   **b)** ticklish

     c) hopefully   **d)** hopeless

     e) greatness   **f)** expectant

6 marks

5. Choose the correct word to complete each sentence below.

unkind   prevent   misunder-stand

a) How can you _____ such a clear instruction?

b) He was _____ to his friend.

c) They had to _____ the accident from occurring.

3 marks

6. Insert the correct prefix to make the root word make sense in each of these sentences.

a) They were sent back to ____take their test.

b) The parents were stuck in traffic and were ____able to collect their children.

c) The magician made the hat ____appear.

d) They were ____presenting their country at the Olympics.

e) They travelled to the bottom of the ocean in a ____marine.

5 marks

7. Underline the correct homophone in each sentence.

a) A **draught / draft** was coming from under the door.

b) They went to the **bridal / bridle** shop to buy a wedding dress.

c) Camels are good at walking across the **desert / dessert**.

d) They ate rhubard crumble for **desert / dessert**.

e) The bride walked joyfully down the **isle / I'll / aisle**.

5 marks

G **8.** Draw a line to link each word with its synonym.

| flat | large | small | trot | fast |

| jog | little | smooth | quick | big |

5 marks

G **9.** Complete the table to show the synonym and antonym for each word. The first one has been done for you.

Word	Synonym	Antonym
pretty	*beautiful*	*ugly*
work		
open		
tired		

6 marks

10. Write the story genre that fits each description.

a) contains spaceships, aliens and time travel   _____

b) the characters go and explore somewhere   _____

c) there is something that needs solving   _____

3 marks

11. Read the text and answer the questions.

Victorian schools were uninviting places. The windows would be high up so the children could not see out. Unlike your classroom, Victorian classrooms were unattractive and drab; there was very little on the walls apart from a text about behaviour and attitude. Boys and girls were usually separated; schools had separate entrances and playgrounds for each gender.

The classes were very big – one was recorded as having 300 boys in it! The schools in villages would have been smaller but would have a large range of ages in one class. Due to the huge numbers in a class, the teaching was very regimented. A teacher would write on a blackboard and the pupils would copy onto their slates. They would also have to learn a lot of things by continual repetition.

a) What two things did schools have to keep boys and girls separate?

_____

_____

b) What was different about the walls of Victorian classrooms?

_____

c) Did all schools have huge numbers of pupils in? Explain your answer.

_____

_____

d) What did children write on in Victorian schools?

_____

e) Did the children work in groups in Victorian schools? Explain your answer.

_____

_____

f) Would you like to have gone to school in Victorian times? Explain your answer.

_____

_____

6 marks

Marks......... /51

Prefixes

G Grammar   P Punctuation   S Spelling

Challenge 1

S **1** Circle the correct spelling of each of these words.

a) mistake / misstake / misttake

b) preeview / preview / preveiw

c) disttrust / disstrust / distrust

d) rettake / re-take / retake

e) unnhurt / unhurt / unhurtt

5 marks

Marks.......... /5

Challenge 2

If a root word starts with 'l' then the prefix **il-** is added instead of **in-**. If a root word starts with 'r', the prefix **ir-** is added instead of **in-**.

S **1** Write the correct prefix to be used with each root word. Then write the final word that is created.

a) _____ + logical = _____

b) _____ + active = _____

c) _____ + regular = _____

d) _____ + action = _____

e) _____ + literate = _____

f) _____ + capable = _____

g) _____ + visible = _____

h) _____ + legal = _____

i) _____ + replaceable = _____

9 marks

Marks.......... /9

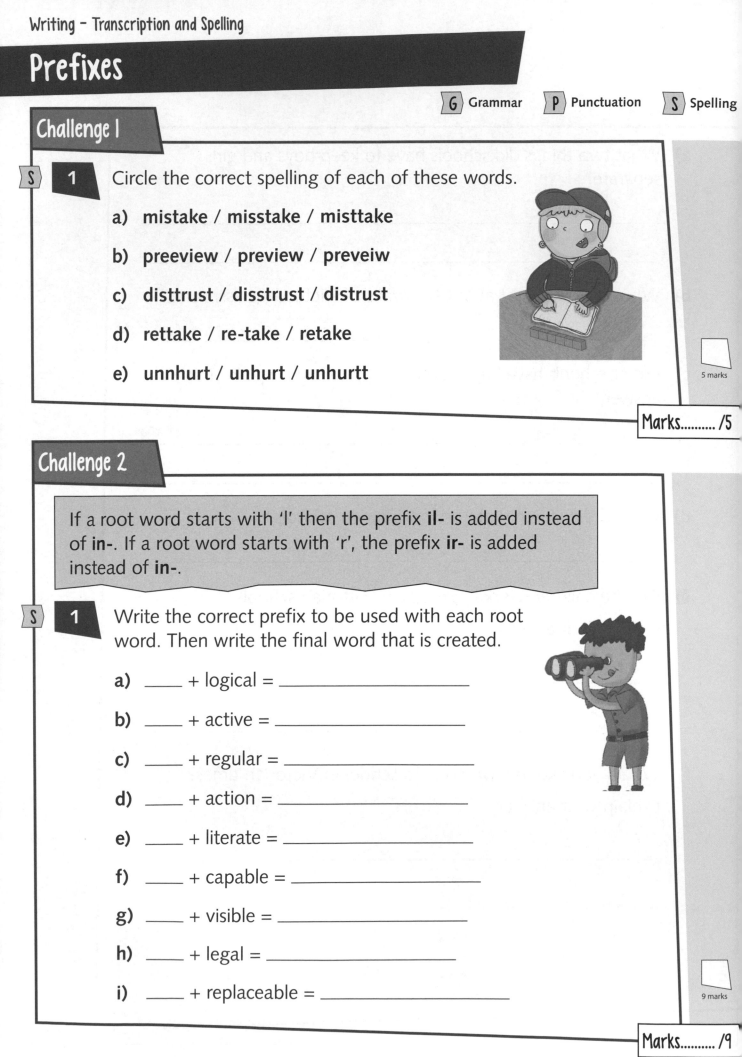

Prefixes

Challenge 3

1 Draw a line to match each prefix to its meaning.

| im- | re- | sub- | super- | anti- |

against   above / over   not   again   under

5 marks

2 Choose the correct prefix to complete the words in these sentences so they make sense.

im-   re-   sub-   super-   anti-

a) We had to _____merge the sponge into the water.

b) It was _____possible to see anything in the distance as it was so misty.

c) Thankfully, the mother was _____united with her son after he had gone missing.

d) The children had a _____natural experience when they pretended to visit aliens from another planet.

e) Sophie was given _____biotics when she went to the doctors.

f) The children were _____turning from their trip late in the evening.

g) They managed to find the right _____dote to reverse the effect of the snake bite.

h) The _____title on the page explained what the paragraph was about.

8 marks

Marks......... /13

Total marks .... /27   How am I doing?   😊   😐   😣

Suffixes

Challenge 1

S **1** Circle the correct spelling in each set of words.

a) furniture / furneture / furnitture

b) hapily / happly / happily

c) gently / gentlely / gentley

d) tention / tension / tenssion

e) acsion / acssion / action

f) dangerrous / dangerous / dangerouss

g) precious / pretious / preccious

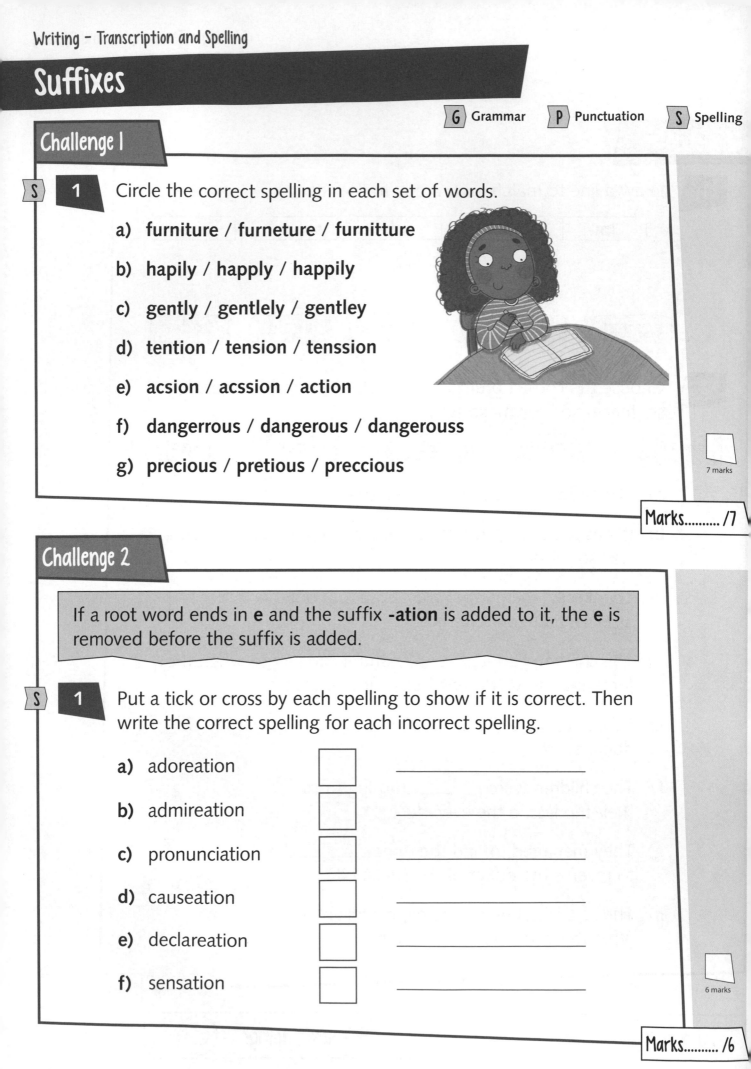

7 marks

Marks.........../7

Challenge 2

If a root word ends in **e** and the suffix **-ation** is added to it, the **e** is removed before the suffix is added.

S **1** Put a tick or cross by each spelling to show if it is correct. Then write the correct spelling for each incorrect spelling.

a) adoreation ☐ _____

b) admireation ☐ _____

c) pronunciation ☐ _____

d) causeation ☐ _____

e) declareation ☐ _____

f) sensation ☐ _____

6 marks

Marks.........../6

Suffixes

Challenge 3

When you add a suffix that **begins with a vowel** to a word of more than one syllable, you sometimes **double the final consonant** of the root word. For example, travel + ed = trave__ll__ed.

1 Write the correct spelling for each of these words when the suffixes shown are added – remember to apply the rule above **only** when the root word has **more than one syllable**.

a) forgot + en _____

b) visit + ed _____

c) listen + ing _____

d) prefer + ed _____

e) begin + ing _____

f) travel + ing _____

6 marks

If a root word ends with **fer**, you **double** the final 'r' of the root word if the **fer** is still **stressed** when the suffix is added:
for example, re**fer** + ed = re**fer**red.
You **do not** double the final 'r' if the **fer** is **not** stressed when the suffix is added:
for example, re**fer** + ence = re**fer**ence.

2 Write the correct spelling for each of these words when the suffixes shown are added:

a) refer + al _____

b) transfer + ing _____

c) transfer + ence _____

d) offer + ed _____

e) prefer + ed _____

5 marks

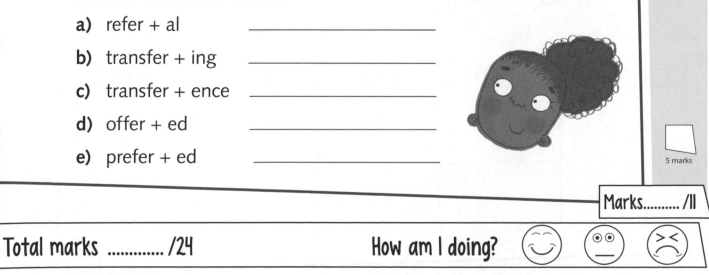

Marks.......... /11

Total marks .... /24   How am I doing?   😊   😐   😣

53

Silent Letters

Challenge 1

S **1** Some words are particularly tricky to spell as they have silent letters. In Old English, these letters were sounded but nowadays they are not. In each of the words below, circle the silent letter.

Example: dou(b)t

a) island

b) glisten

c) wrote

d) solemn

e) knock

f) hymn

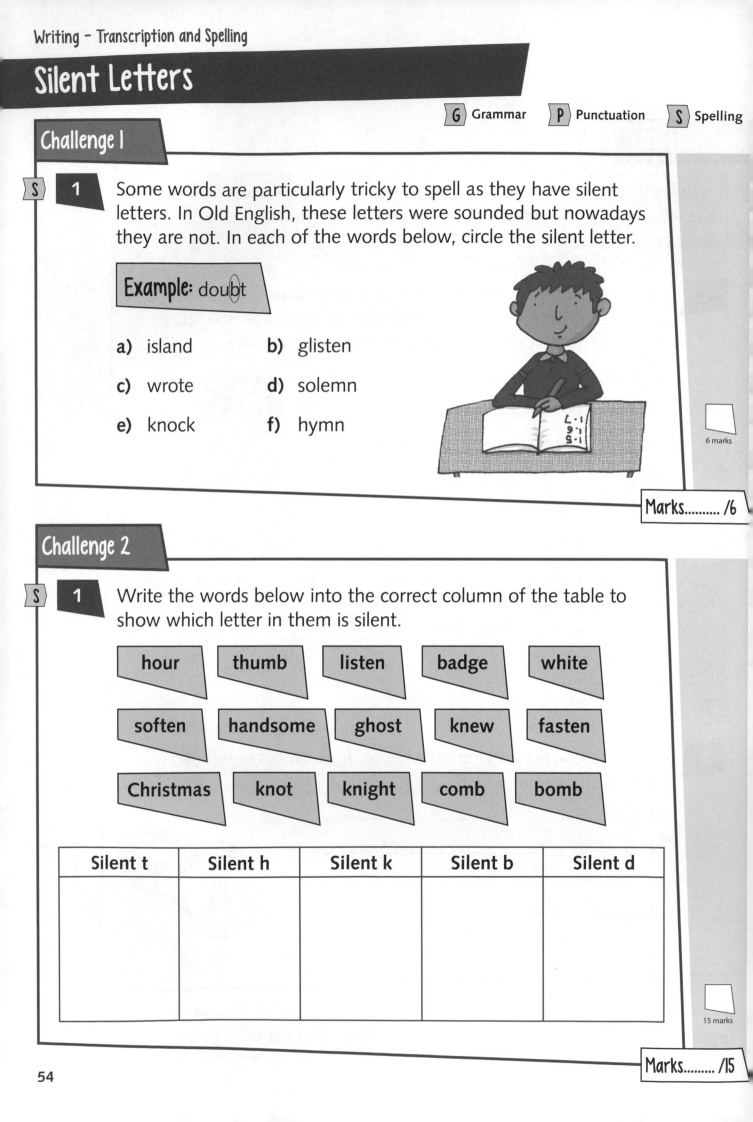

6 marks

Marks.......... /6

Challenge 2

S **1** Write the words below into the correct column of the table to show which letter in them is silent.

| hour | thumb | listen | badge | white |

| soften | handsome | ghost | knew | fasten |

| Christmas | knot | knight | comb | bomb |

Silent t	Silent h	Silent k	Silent b	Silent d

15 marks

Marks......... /15

Silent Letters

Challenge 3

1 Read each sentence and fill in the missing silent letter to make the word correct.

a) I clim____ed to the top of the hill.

b) I wrote the numbers in a colum____.

c) I was able to b____ild a tower out of the bricks.

d) The biscuit crum____s were all over the table.

e) The king and queen lived in a cas____le.

f) I learn lots of things when I go to sc____ool.

g) Can you g____ess who is behind the door?

h) Arthur pulled the s____ord from the stone.

i) After summer it is autum____.

j) The r____inoceros charged at the tractor.

10 marks

Marks.........../10

Total marks ..../31   How am I doing?

Homophones

Challenge 1

SG 1 Circle the correct word to complete the sentences.

a) The stars were shining in the dark **night / knight**.

b) It was fun to **meat / meet** my new baby sister.

c) I was allowed to **bye / buy / by** some sweets at the shop.

d) There was **dew / due** on the grass in the morning.

e) The hotel **maid / made** tidied the room for us.

f) I found the book hard to **read / reed**.

g) It was **their / there / they're** turn to play on the climbing frame.

7 marks

Marks.......... /7

Challenge 2

SG 1 Match the correct pairs of homophones by drawing lines between them.

bear	sore
blew	pour
plane	plain
hare	bare
paw	here
new	blue
hear	hair
saw	knew

8 marks

Homophones

2 Use some of the homophones from Challenge 2, question 1 to complete the sentences below.

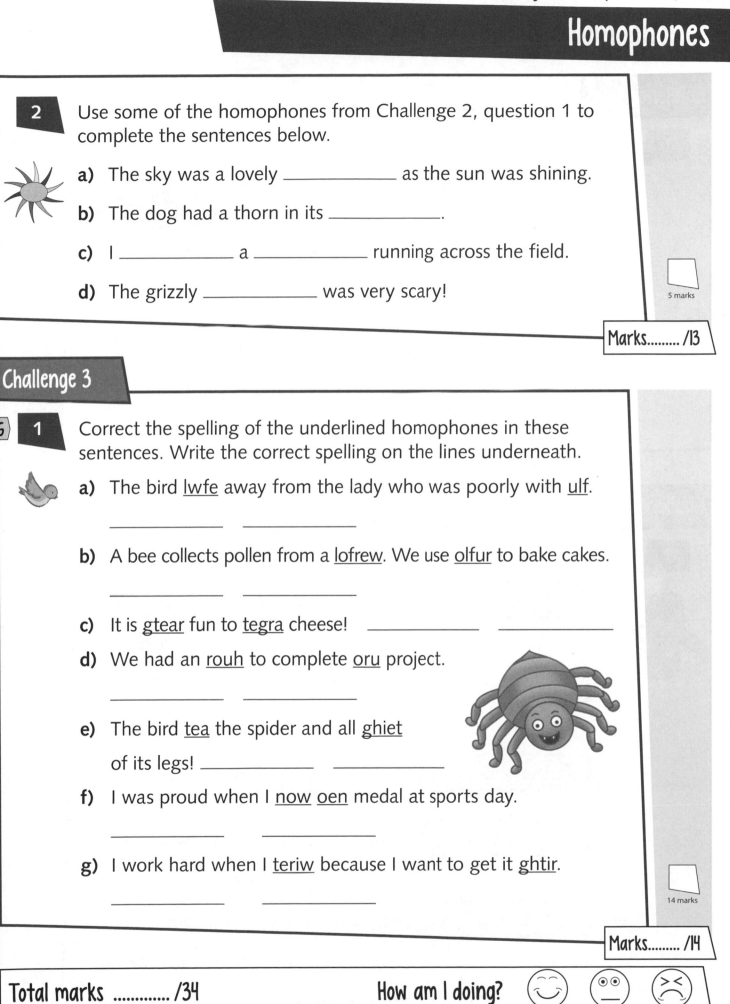

a) The sky was a lovely _____ as the sun was shining.

b) The dog had a thorn in its _____.

c) I _____ a _____ running across the field.

d) The grizzly _____ was very scary!

5 marks

Marks.........../13

Challenge 3

1 Correct the spelling of the underlined homophones in these sentences. Write the correct spelling on the lines underneath.

a) The bird <u>lwfe</u> away from the lady who was poorly with <u>ulf</u>.

_____   _____

b) A bee collects pollen from a <u>lofrew</u>. We use <u>olfur</u> to bake cakes.

_____   _____

c) It is <u>gtear</u> fun to <u>tegra</u> cheese!   _____   _____

d) We had an <u>rouh</u> to complete <u>oru</u> project.

_____   _____

e) The bird <u>tea</u> the spider and all <u>ghiet</u>

of its legs! _____   _____

f) I was proud when I <u>now</u> <u>oen</u> medal at sports day.

_____   _____

g) I work hard when I <u>teriw</u> because I want to get it <u>ghtir</u>.

_____   _____

14 marks

Marks.........../14

Total marks ..../34   How am I doing?   😊   😐   😣

Confusing Words

G Grammar   P Punctuation   S Spelling

Challenge 1

SG 1 Underline the correct word in each sentence.

a) My teacher gave me a good piece of **advice / advise**.

b) They had to **device / devise** a cunning plan to escape.

c) I did lots of piano **practice / practise** last night.

d) We had to **proceed / precede** with our plan.

e) Pens, pencils and scissors live in my **stationary / stationery** drawer.

5 marks

Marks.......... /5

Challenge 2

SG 1 Put the correct word in each gap in these sentences.

a) **who's / whose**   Can I ask _____ responsible

for finding out _____ coat it is?

b) **wary / weary**   You should be _____ of lions

when they are _____ and wanting to sleep.

c) **farther / father**   My _____ ran _____ than my mother.

d) **passed / past**   In the _____ year my brother

_____ his driving test.

e) **led / lead**   The _____ on the roof

_____ the thief to the building.

10 marks

Confusing Words

2 Write a sentence that contains both of these words.

(**guest / guessed**) _____

_____

2 marks

Marks......... /12

Challenge 3

1 Read the passage and underline the words that have been used incorrectly.

> I would advice you to listen carefully to the advise you are given about how a guessed must behave when at a hotel. My farther says that you must not wake up too early in the mourning and if you do you should be quite. If you have an electronic devise like an iPad then you should turn the volume down.

7 marks

2 Write the correct word for each of the words you have underlined in question 1 above.

a) _____

b) _____

c) _____

d) _____

e) _____

f) _____

g) _____

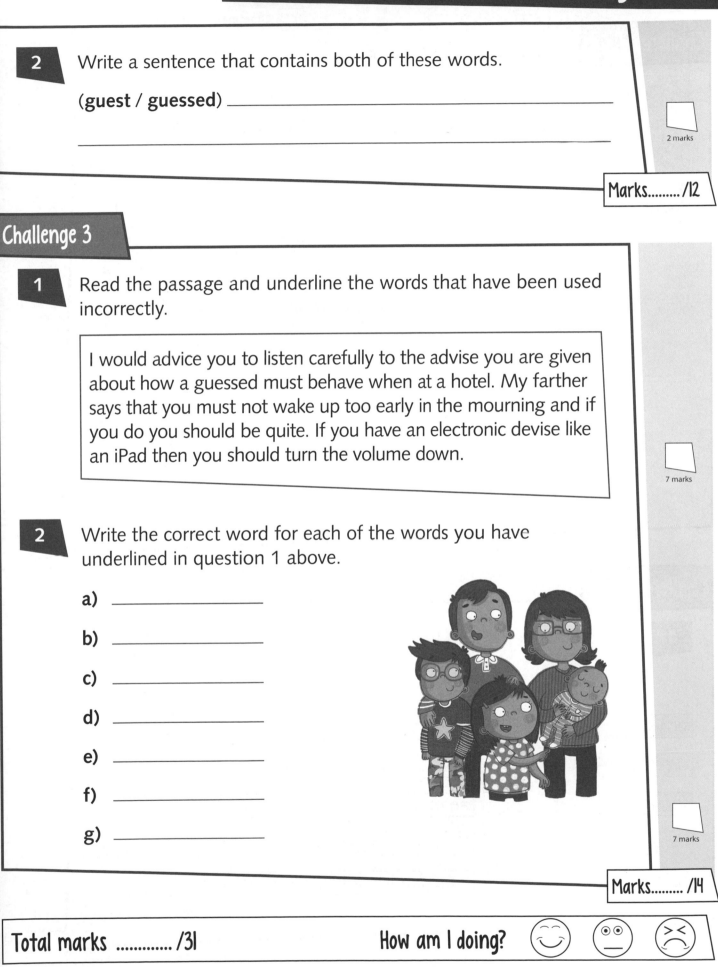

7 marks

Marks......... /14

Total marks .... /31   How am I doing?   😊   😐   😣

Using a Dictionary

Challenge 1

In a dictionary words are organised in alphabetical order. If words start with the same letter, they are put in order using the first two or three letters.

S **1** Put these words in the order they would appear in a dictionary.

| vehicle | bargain | opportunity | ancient |

| forty | occur | vegetable | familiar |

a) _____   b) _____

c) _____   d) _____

e) _____   f) _____

g) _____   h) _____

8 marks

Marks.......... /8

Challenge 2

S **1** Match the words with their meanings by drawing lines between them. Use a dictionary to help you if needed.

bruise	a person who is in the army
dictionary	from a country different from your own
foreign	an injury shown as discoloured skin
neighbour	a book listing words / meanings of a language
soldier	a person living next door or near

5 marks

Marks.......... /5

Using a Dictionary

Challenge 3

1 The word **game** has a number of different meanings. Here are three of them:

> 1 *(noun)* competitive activity or sport played using rules
>
> 2 *(noun)* an activity someone does for fun
>
> 3 *(adjective)* eager to try something new

Choose the correct definition number to explain how the word **game** is used in the following sentences. Write the number.

a) The computer **game** was fun to play. _____

b) The tennis **game** was gripping. _____

c) He was **game** to try and climb the tower. _____

3 marks

2 Use a dictionary to look up the following words. Write a definition in your own words to show the meaning of each word.

a) government _____

_____

b) yacht _____

_____

2 marks

Marks.......... /5

Total marks .... /18   How am I doing? 😊 😐 😣

Using a Thesaurus

Challenge 1

The words in a thesaurus, like in a dictionary, are listed in alphabetical order.

G **1** Look at the words below and arrange them into the order they would appear in a thesaurus.

| happy | content | pleased | joyful |

| cheerful | jolly | merry |

a) _____   b) _____

c) _____   d) _____

e) _____   f) _____

g) _____

7 marks

Marks.......... /7

Challenge 2

A thesaurus gives you words that are the same or similar in meaning to the one you have looked up (synonyms).

G **1** Here are some words from a thesaurus. Choose the word that you feel fits the sentence best from the choice given.

help: aid, support, assistance
said: thought, whispered

a) James _____ something quietly to Sam.

b) They had to call for roadside _____.

c) She _____ hard about the answer.

d) I asked for some _____ to complete the work.

4 marks

Marks.......... /4

Using a Thesaurus

Challenge 3

1 Circle the word that can replace the underlined word in each sentence.

a) It was a <u>wet</u> (**bright / rainy / pleasant**) day so all the animals were huddling for shelter.

b) "Stop right there!" <u>said</u> (**shouted / whispered / asked**) the policeman.

c) The money was <u>secure</u> (**open / stolen / safe**) as it was locked in the safe.

d) I <u>ran</u> (**limped / jogged / cycled**) to the shops to buy some sweets.

e) The animals <u>froze</u> (**ran / cried / stopped**) when they saw the fire in the bushes.

5 marks

2 Complete the passage below by choosing the correct synonyms from this word bank to replace the underlined words.

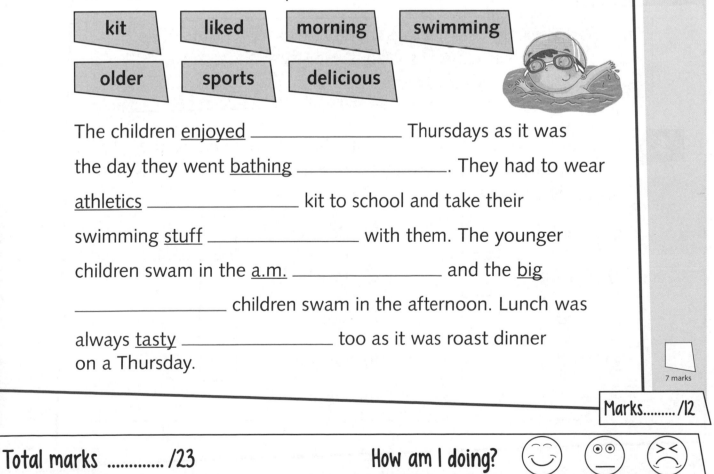

kit   liked   morning   swimming

older   sports   delicious

The children <u>enjoyed</u> _____ Thursdays as it was

the day they went <u>bathing</u> _____. They had to wear

<u>athletics</u> _____ kit to school and take their

swimming <u>stuff</u> _____ with them. The younger

children swam in the <u>a.m.</u> _____ and the <u>big</u>

_____ children swam in the afternoon. Lunch was

always <u>tasty</u> _____ too as it was roast dinner
on a Thursday.

7 marks

Marks.........../12

Total marks .... /23   How am I doing? 😊 😐 😖

Tricky Spellings

G Grammar   P Punctuation   S Spelling

Challenge 1

Some words are particularly tricky to spell as they have 'silent' letters in them. Hundreds of years ago these letters would have been sounded out but they are not today (making them tricky to spell).

S 1 Underline the **silent** letter in each of the following words.

a) reign   **b)** doubt

c) thistle   **d)** knight

e) comb   **f)** hymn

g) design   **h)** know

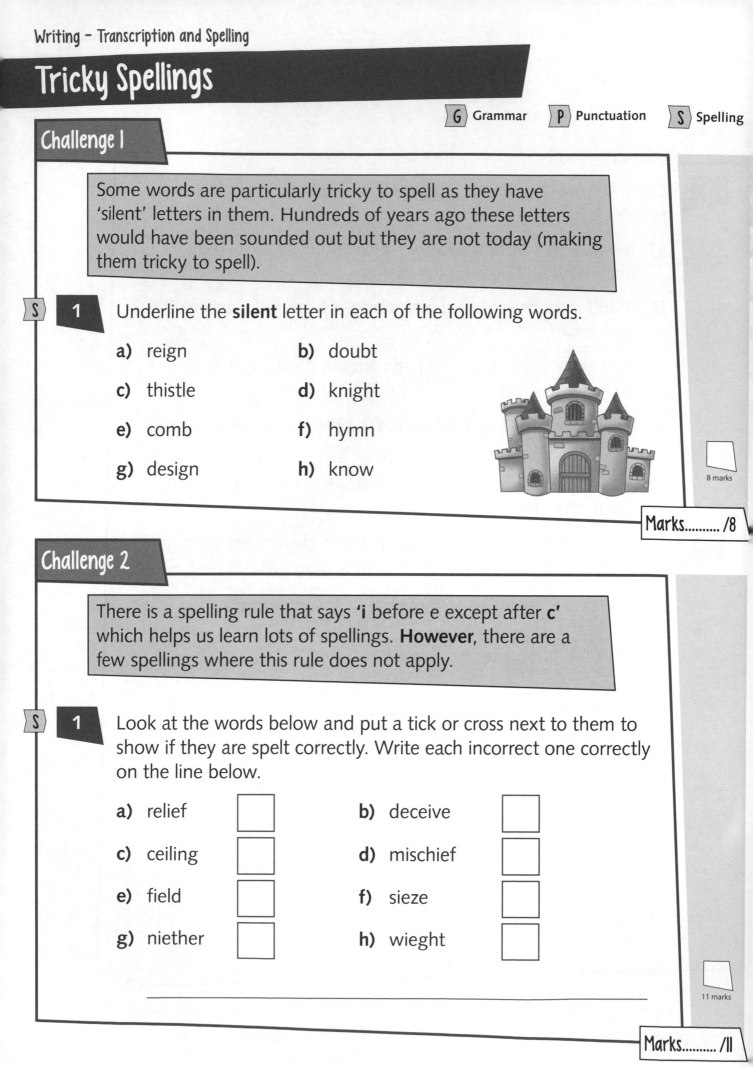

8 marks

Marks.......... /8

Challenge 2

There is a spelling rule that says '**i** before e except after **c**' which helps us learn lots of spellings. **However**, there are a few spellings where this rule does not apply.

S 1 Look at the words below and put a tick or cross next to them to show if they are spelt correctly. Write each incorrect one correctly on the line below.

a) relief ☐   **b)** deceive ☐

c) ceiling ☐   **d)** mischief ☐

e) field ☐   **f)** sieze ☐

g) niether ☐   **h)** wieght ☐

_____

11 marks

Marks.......... /11

Tricky Spellings

Challenge 3

1 Underline the correct spelling for the word given in each sentence.

a) I went to visit an **ancient / anceint / aincient** historical site yesterday.

b) The **goverment / government / govermment** makes decisions about how our country is run.

c) I had to **que / kew / queue** for a long time at the ice-cream van.

d) The teacher told us not to **interrupt / interupt / interuppt** her when she was speaking.

e) My swimming coach said I was doing **excellant / excelent / excellent** work in my training.

f) We had a gymnastics **competition / comppetition / compettition** at my club yesterday.

g) I had the **oporrtunity / opportunity / oporttunity** to go skiing with my class.

h) The monkeys at the zoo were very **mischeivious / mischievious / mischievous**.

i) The lion was very **agressive / aggressive / aggresive** when the meat was thrown into his cage.

j) They could not **guarantee / guarrantee / guaranntee** that I would get a place on the skiing trip.

k) The school hall could **acommodate / accomodate / accommodate** 450 people.

l) The **committee / comittee / commitee** voted to buy new playground equipment for the school.

12 marks

Marks.........../12

Total marks ..../31   How am I doing?   ☺   ☻   ☹

Progress Test 2

S) 1. Circle the correct spelling of each of these words.

    a) bargin / bargain / bargen

    b) fourty / forty / forrty

    c) harass / harrass / herrass

    d) temprature / temparature / temperature

    e) cureiosity / curiosity / curriosity

5 marks

S) 2. Write the correct prefix from the ones below. Then write the final word that is created.

    il   ir   in

    a) _____ + take = _____

    b) _____ + regular = _____

    c) _____ + legal = _____

    d) _____ + complete = _____

4 marks

S) 3. Put a tick next to the words that are spelt correctly. Put a cross next to the incorrect words and write each corrected spelling.

    a) profesion   ☐   _____

    b) pronunciasion   ☐   _____

    c) hesitation   ☐   _____

    d) observeation   ☐   _____

    e) confession   ☐   _____

5 marks

4. Add the missing silent letters to each of these words to make them correct.

a) lam_____   **b)** dou_____t   **c)** this_____le

3 marks

5. Write a homophone for each of these words.

a) new   _____

b) saw   _____

c) aisle   _____

3 marks

6. Circle the correct word in each sentence.

a) I had to **alter / altar** my design.

b) They had to **bow / bough** at the end of the play.

c) A **prophet / profit** is someone who foretells the future.

3 marks

7. Write these words in the correct order as they would appear in a dictionary.

| soldier | sacrifice | suggest | symbol | secretary | system |

a) _____   **b)** _____

c) _____   **d)** _____

e) _____   **f)** _____

6 marks

8. Circle the word that can replace the one underlined in the sentence.

a) It was a <u>cold</u> (**bright / uncaring / chilly**) day on Sunday so we all wore our coats.

b) "I had a fantastic time today!" <u>shouted</u> (**wailed / bellowed / whispered**) Freya.

c) The <u>team</u> (**squad / individual / friends**) played well during the match.

3 marks

S **9.** Put a tick by each word spelt correctly and a cross by each word that is incorrect. Write each correct spelling on the line provided.

a) anceint ☐ _____

b) consceince ☐ _____

c) convenience ☐ _____

d) sufficeint ☐ _____

e) science ☐ _____

5 marks

10. Read these extracts and circle the genre you think each comes from.

a)

> I wandered lonely as a cloud
>
> That floats on high o'er vales and hills,
>
> When all at once I saw a crowd,
>
> A host, of golden daffodils:

diary / instructions / biography / newspaper / poetry

b)

> What a rubbish day! First, I had a maths test (which I had forgotten to revise for) and then we had double English and I got told off for talking. I knew it would be a horrid day cos I didn't get to sleep early enough last night...

diary / instructions / biography / newspaper / poetry

2 marks

11. Circle the meaning of the root word shown in the word family given.

> root word: <u>graph</u>
>
> word family: graphic, phonograph, graphite

meaning: **good** / **light** / **writing** / **place**

1 mark

12. Insert the correct suffix to make the root word make sense in each of these sentences. You may have to change the spelling of some root words.

a) The excite_____ was electric in the stadium.

b) The rabbit had hurt his leg and lay help_____ in the field.

c) They had to find a film suit_____ for children to watch.

d) The children had to be sense_____ in the line.

e) They travel_____ a long way on the first day of the journey.

5 marks

13. Write the correct prefix to be used and the final word that is created.

a) _____ + complete = _____

b) _____ + correct = _____

c) _____ + legible = _____

d) _____ + definite = _____

e) _____ + relevant = _____

5 marks

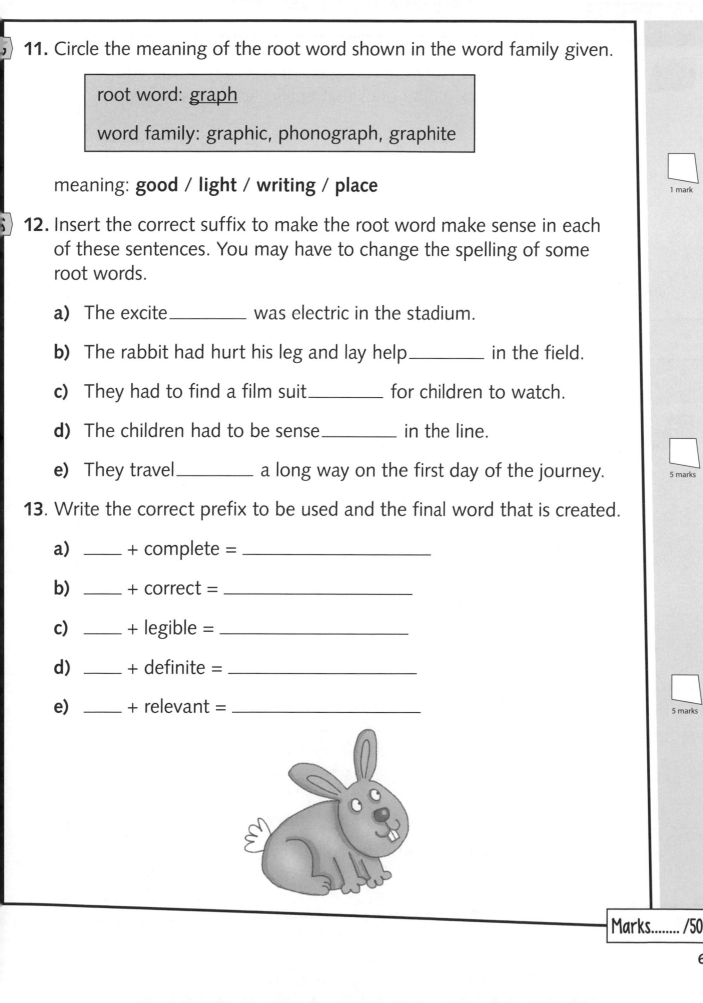

Marks........ /50

Audience and Purpose

G Grammar   P Punctuation   S Spelling

Challenge 1

1   If you were writing a story for young children, what would you need to include? Tick all the ones that apply. Add crosses for those that don't apply.

a) simple language ☐   b) long sentences ☐

c) exciting pictures ☐   d) simple story structure ☐

e) chapters ☐   f) lots of characters ☐

g) exciting story plot ☐

7 marks

Marks.......... /7

Challenge 2

1   For each example below, circle the genre and the purpose of the writing.

a)
> I am writing to you to inform you of my decision to leave the school. It has not been an easy decision as I love my job, but I have been offered the chance to go and teach in China.

Genre: **recount / advert / letter / story**

Purpose: **persuasion / information / complaint**

b)
> Jigglepops are the new, sensational breakfast cereal that all the cool kids (and grown-ups) are queuing up for. Not only do they taste great, they are really good for you too! Can you really afford not to give them a go? Available in all major supermarkets.

Genre: **recount / advert / letter / story**

Purpose: **persuasion / information / complaint**

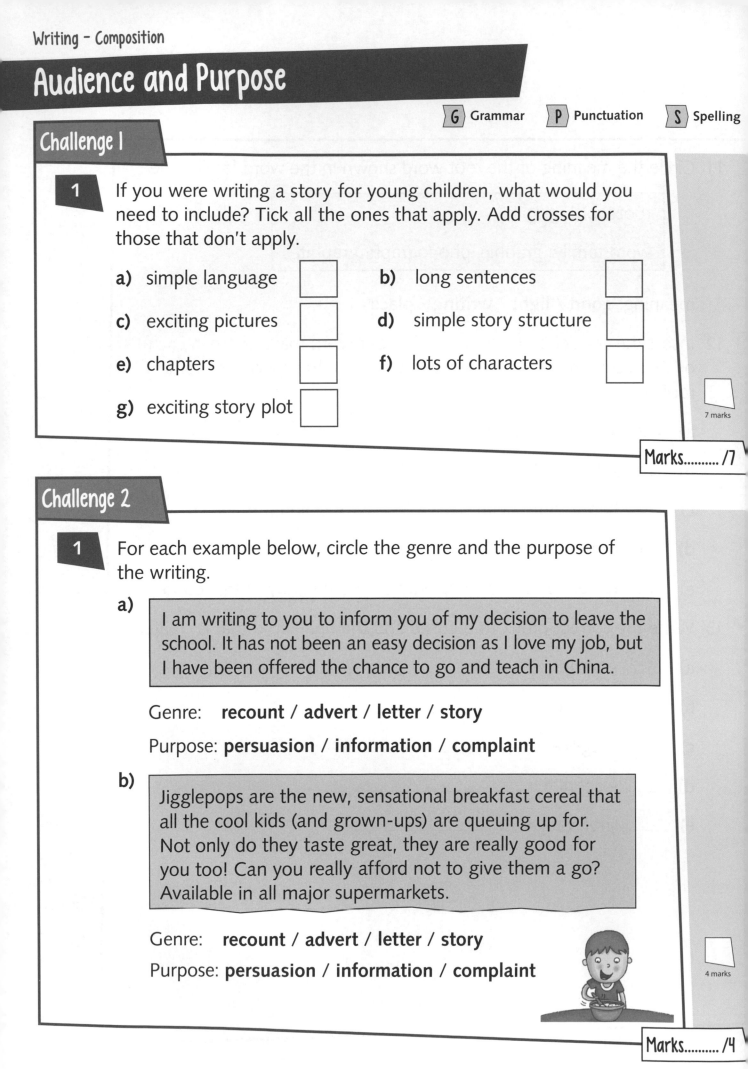

4 marks

Marks.......... /4

Audience and Purpose

1 Read the extracts and circle the most appropriate audience and genre.

a)

> There was once a rabbit called Boris. He liked to eat carrots. He lived in a burrow with his family. He loved to go on adventures.

Audience: **adults / teenagers / young children**

Genre: **story / recount / letter**

b)

> Because of the hot summer weather, please ensure that your child comes to school with a sun hat and sun lotion. If possible, please put 24-hour sun lotion on them in the morning so that they do not have to worry about reapplying during the day.

Audience: **adults / teenagers / young children**

Genre: **story / recount / letter**

c)

> Bruce stepped gingerly through the portal; he had no idea what he was going to see in front of him when he opened his eyes. He felt a mixture of tension, fear and excitement. It was fear that gripped him once he opened his eyes…

Audience: **adults / teenagers / young children**

Genre: **story / recount / letter**

6 marks

Marks.......... /6

Total marks .... /17   How am I doing? 😊 😐 😣

Different Forms of Writing

Challenge 1

1 Writing takes many different forms. Write each genre into the correct column of the table to show if it is fiction or non-fiction.

advert   story   picture book   biography

recount   report   explanation   comic

Fiction	Non-fiction

8 marks

Marks.......... /8

Challenge 2

1 **Tick** each feature that you might see in an advert. Put a **cross** by each one you would **not** see.

a) rhetorical questions ☐   b) humour ☐

c) long paragraphs ☐   d) memorable slogan ☐

e) numbered steps ☐   f) tempting descriptions ☐

g) quotes from customers ☐   h) address in top right corner ☐

i) special offers ☐   j) prices ☐

10 marks

Marks......... /10

Different Forms of Writing

Challenge 3

1 Read each extract and circle the genre.

a)
> Roald Dahl was born on 13th September 1916 in South Wales. His parents were Norwegian and he spent many of his summers visiting his grandparents in Oslo…

recount / autobiography / biography / report

b)
> Polar bears are the largest land-based carnivores in the whole world. They are strong swimmers and therefore their Arctic home is perfect as it allows them to be around water for much of their life. They have a thick coat and layer of fat, which keeps them warm and camouflaged…

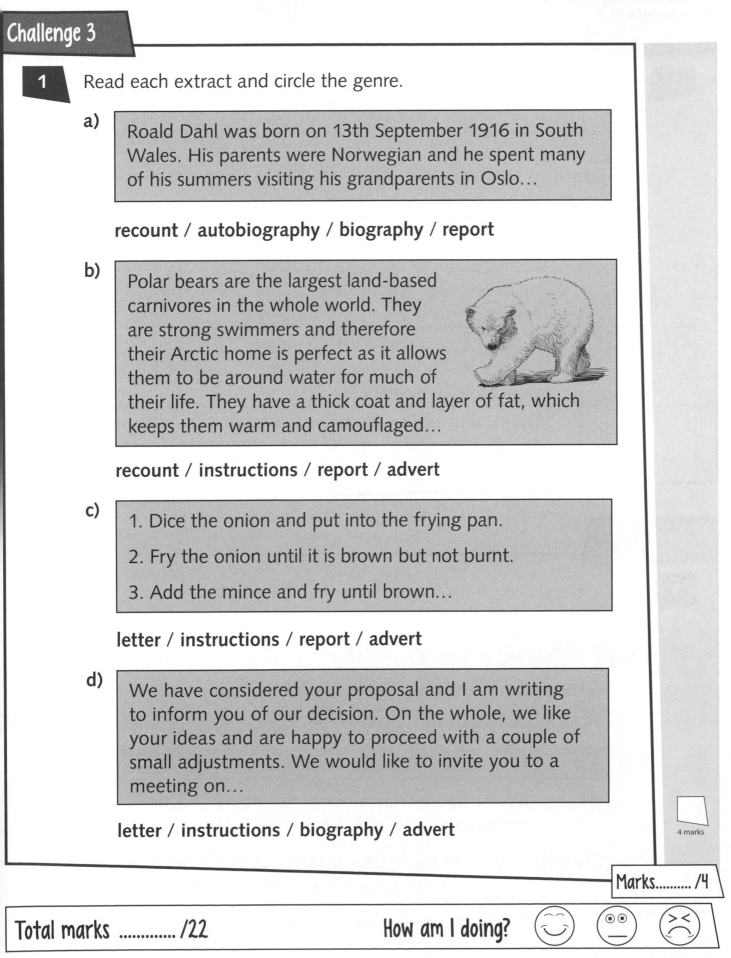

recount / instructions / report / advert

c)
> 1. Dice the onion and put into the frying pan.
> 2. Fry the onion until it is brown but not burnt.
> 3. Add the mince and fry until brown…

letter / instructions / report / advert

d)
> We have considered your proposal and I am writing to inform you of our decision. On the whole, we like your ideas and are happy to proceed with a couple of small adjustments. We would like to invite you to a meeting on…

letter / instructions / biography / advert

4 marks

Marks.........../4

Total marks ..../22   How am I doing? 😊 😐 😣

Developing Characters and Settings

 G Grammar   **P** Punctuation   **S** Spelling

Challenge 1

1 From your knowledge of characters in storybooks, write the character name at the beginning of the row that matches the description from a story.

(**pirate**)   (**mermaid**)   (**princess**)

Character	Description
a)	She sat elegantly on her high-backed chair in the throne room. Her dress was exquisite and her jewels shone brilliantly.
b)	He gripped his sword with his three fingers and thumb. He had one eye and a lopsided grin. His eyes were as cold as the ocean.
c)	She sat elegantly on the rock. Her beautiful sandy hair flowed down to her waist where her beautiful tail began.

3 marks

Marks............/3

Challenge 2

1 Circle the setting(s) and character(s) you think each of these stories could have.

a) A story set in Tudor times about a king who had lots of wives.

Settings: **farm / beach / castle / swimming pool / village**

Characters: **Henry VIII / jester / DJ / ladies / bishop**

7 marks

b) A story set in Victorian times about a child who works for a living.

Settings: **manor house / farm / cinema / dusty streets / motorway**

Characters: **Lady of the Manor / traffic warden / butler / street urchins / teacher / bus conductor**

6 marks

Marks........../13

Developing Characters and Settings

Challenge 3

1 Read the extracts and circle the setting that is being described.

a)
> The golden sand glinted in the sun. The tiny waves lapping on the shore made the smallest of sounds. Simon lay back and closed his eyes. This was as near to perfect as any place he could think of...

cinema / swimming pool / **beach** / school / park

b)
> The smell of chlorine wafted out as soon as the automatic doors opened. The echoes of the children's excited voices could be heard. Mum knew that she would have to endure it because Siobhan loved splashing in the water and it was for her that they had come...

cinema / **swimming pool** / beach / school / park

c)
> The desks were arranged differently from normal. They were usually grouped together so that the children could work in groups but today they were set up individually. All of the desks were in lines facing the front with only one chair at each of them. Today must be the day of the SATs test...

cinema / swimming pool / beach / **school** / park

d)
> She swung dismally on the swing. She was sure the others had said they would meet her here – where were they? She had already had three goes on the zip wire but it just wasn't the same on her own without her friends...

cinema / swimming pool / beach / school / **park**

4 marks

Marks.......... /4

Total marks .... /20   How am I doing? 😊 😐 😣

Using Dialogue

Challenge 1

P   **1**   Rewrite each piece of dialogue, putting the speech marks in correctly.

a) Hazel said, Please can I come too?

_____

b) Do you believe me? Phoebe asked.

_____

c) Believe it or not, Tim said, it's true!

_____

d) Stop, the teacher shouted. You need to listen to me!

_____

4 marks

Marks.......... /4

Challenge 2

G   **1**   Turn each of these sentences into direct speech.

a) Mum said it was her birthday today.

_____

b) The teacher told the class to stop talking now.

_____

c) William said he would see me later.

_____

d) Oscar said he had to leave immediately.

_____

4 marks

Marks.......... /4

Using Dialogue

Challenge 3

1 Write the missing punctuation in this box.

> The sand, remarked Grace, is very soft and warm on my feet.
>
> I know, replied Sandjit. It is lovely isn't it?
>
> Shall we paddle in the sea? asked Grace.
>
> Sounds fun, replied Sandjit, but do you think it will be as warm as the sand?
>
> I doubt it, answered Grace, but we can always warm our feet on the sand again.
>
> Let's go! shouted Sandjit and Grace together.

6 marks

2 Continue this short dialogue between two people where they each say two additional things. Put the correct speech marks in.

> "Hello Mark," exclaimed Tim. "How are you today?"
> "Hi Tim," replied Mark. "I am really well thank you. How about you?"

_____

_____

_____

_____

_____

_____

_____

4 marks

Marks......... /10

Total marks .... /18   How am I doing?   😊   😐   😣

Organising your Writing

Challenge 1

1 When planning a story, you need to think about things in the right order. Label each part 1–6 to show the order the plan should be written in.

a) story opening ☐

b) story ending ☐

c) characters that will be in it ☐

d) the settings in the story ☐

e) the main event ☐

f) the build-up ☐

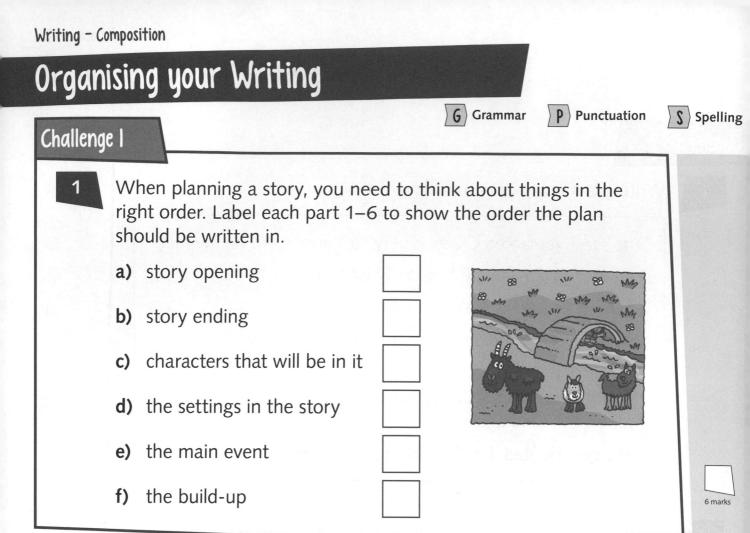

6 marks

Marks.......... /6

Challenge 2

1 Here is the story plan for a well-known story. Write the order that the events happen in, from 1–8.

a) The wolf eats Granny and puts her clothes on. ☐

b) Little Red Riding Hood sets off to visit Granny. ☐

c) The wolf eats Little Red-Riding Hood and falls asleep. ☐

d) The wolf rattles every time he walks and can't eat any more people. ☐

e) Little Red Riding Hood meets a wolf and tells him where Granny lives. ☐

f) When Little Red Riding Hood arrives at Granny's house she is surprised by her appearance. ☐

Organising your Writing

g) The woodcutter finds the wolf asleep and cuts him open. Little Red Riding Hood and Granny pop out unharmed. ☐

h) Little Red Riding Hood puts stones in the wolf's tummy and sews him up. ☐

10 marks

Marks......... /10

Challenge 3

1 Look at the list of things that a writer needs to think about before, during and after writing. Write each one into the correct column of the table.

A characters	**B** writing in paragraphs
C settings	**D** beginning
E using dialogue	**F** does it make sense?
G range of sentences	**H** is there a beginning, middle and end?
I middle	**J** check spellings
K using a variety of words	**L** check punctuation
M sticking to the plan	**N** end
O main event	**P** audience
Q check grammar	**R** purpose

Before Writing	During Writing	After Writing

18 marks

Marks......... /18

Total marks .... /34   How am I doing? 😊 😐 😣

Editing

Challenge 1

G **1** Underline the grammar mistake in each sentence. Then rewrite each sentence correctly.

a) He were going to the park.

_____

b) They play happily all day at the beach yesterday.

_____

c) It have only just happened.

_____

d) You is in big trouble now.

_____

e) I are going home now.

_____

5 marks

Marks.......... /5

Challenge 2

S **1** Read the passage and underline the **six** spelling mistakes. Spell the words correctly on the lines provided.

It was a hostile enviroment. The trees had branches that whipped back and left bruses on their skin. Harry had agreed to acompany them on this trip but was regretting that decision now. He had to continue though, otherwise there would have been dissasterous consequences. He wondered if he could pursade them to go along a shorter route back to camp. He was desprate to get back quickly so that he could rest and recover.

Editing

a) _____   b) _____

c) _____   d) _____

e) _____   f) _____

6 marks

Marks.......... /6

Challenge 3

SP 1 Read this passage. Underline all the mistakes.
Then write the passage out correctly.

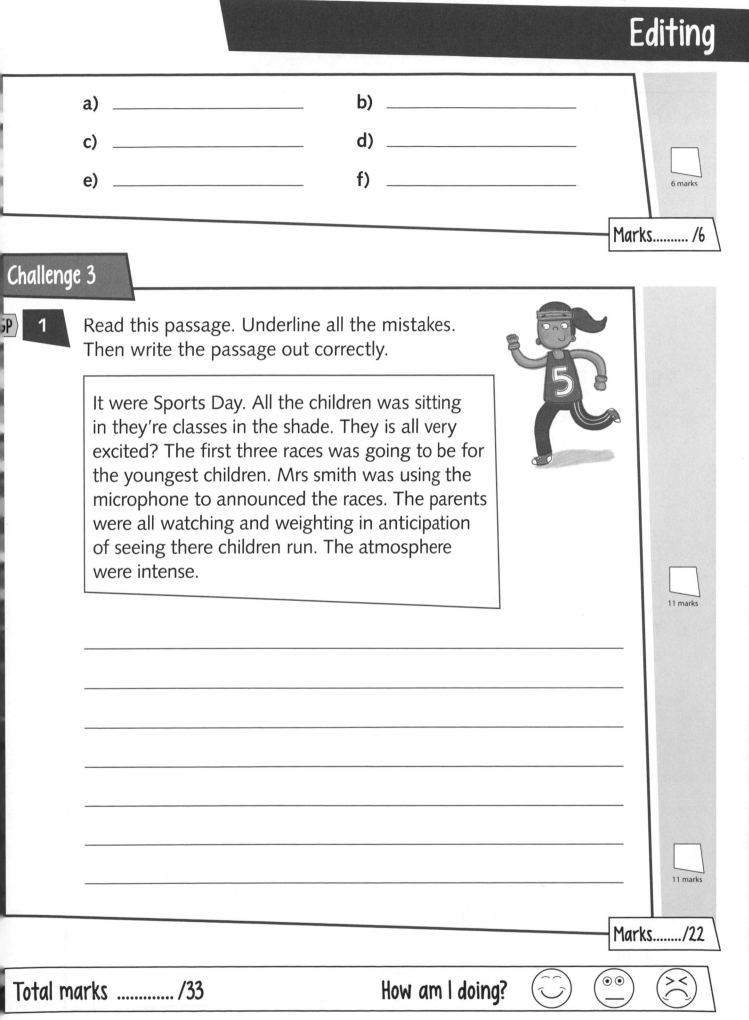

It were Sports Day. All the children was sitting
in they're classes in the shade. They is all very
excited? The first three races was going to be for
the youngest children. Mrs smith was using the
microphone to announced the races. The parents
were all watching and weighting in anticipation
of seeing there children run. The atmosphere
were intense.

11 marks

_____

_____

_____

_____

_____

_____

_____

11 marks

Marks......../22

Total marks ..../33   How am I doing? ☺ 😐 😣

1. Circle the genre and the purpose of writing for each extract.

a)
> The adventurers continued on their way having recovered from their near-death experience. The memories of that experience would live with them forever but for now they had to be brave and courageous. The four children (and their trusty dog) set off towards the mangrove swamps…

Genre: **recount / advert / letter / story**

Purpose of writing: **persuasion / information / complaint / entertain**

b)
> Our trip to Montacue House was amazing. The whole class enjoyed themselves and have done some brilliant work about it. When we arrived I was amazed to see how long the driveway to the house was. The first place we went to (after the toilets) was the Great Hall. The guide showed us around and told us interesting facts…

Genre: **recount / advert / letter / story**

Purpose of writing: **persuasion / information / complaint / entertain**

4 marks

2. Tick the features that you might see in a newspaper report. Put a cross by the ones you would **not** see.

a) questions

b) humour

c) written in columns

d) diagrams

e) numbered steps

f) tempting descriptions

g) quotes

h) address in top right corner ☐

i) captions ☐

j) photo / picture related to writing ☐

☐
10 marks

3. Read the extracts and circle the setting that is being described.

a)

> The happy voices could be heard a long distance away, hovering like bees in the air. The green grass, the football goals, the banks of flowers hit my eyes first. My attention was then drawn to the happy faces playing on the slides, swings, climbing frames and zip wires. It was a hive of activity!

forest / cottage / school / theatre / ice rink / playpark

b)

> My first impression was that the building was old and in need of a lick of paint. It filled me with doubt. Where was I taking my child? Thankfully, the moment we entered the building my impression changed. The walls were bright and colourful, the carpet was clean and new and the people who met us were friendly and smiling.

cinema / swimming pool / beach / school / park

☐
2 marks

4. Turn each of these sentences into direct speech.

a) Hermione wailed that her phone was broken.

_____

b) Fatima announced that her rabbit is called Doris.

_____

c) Murray exclaimed that he needed to lie down.

_____

☐
3 marks

Progress Test 3

Grammar   Punctuation   Spelling

G **5.** Underline the grammar mistake in each sentence. Then rewrite each sentence correctly.

    a) It were time to go home.

    _____

    b) I isn't going to school today.

    _____

4 marks

S **6.** Circle the correct prefix for each word.

    a) **pre / un / mis** represent   **b)** **re / pro / dis** take

    c) **pre / re / sub** inforce   **d)** **re / un / mis** understood

    e) **pro / dis / sub** merge   **f)** **tele / re / mis** phone

6 marks

S **7.** Use the suffixes below to make new words. You may need to change the spelling of the root word before adding the suffix.

-sion   **-ible**

    a) sense _____   **b)** provide _____

    c) defence _____   **d)** horrid _____

    e) tense _____   **f)** decide _____

6 marks

G **8.** Put the correct word into the gaps in these sentences.

    a) **guessed / guest** The wedding _____ was very happy.

    b) **aloud / allowed** The magician said the spell _____.

    c) **complement / compliment** She was given a _____ about her appearance.

3 marks

9. Read each sentence and write an antonym for each word underlined.

    a) They wanted to buy a <u>big</u> house. _____

    b) The horses were <u>restless</u> in their stables. _____

    c) The children were very <u>noisy</u> eating their lunch.

    _____

3 marks

10. Underline the stage directions in this extract.

Mum: *(whispering to Dad)* When is this performance going to end?

Dad: *(waking up from short nap and whispering)* Eh? What? Oh… yes. It's good isn't it?

Mum: *(laughing and whispering)* How would you know? You've been asleep.

Dad: *(sheepishly and quietly)* Only for a few minutes… sorry. It is rather long though isn't it?

4 marks

11. Write the correct word created when each suffix is added to the root word shown.

    a) refer + al = _____

    b) prefer + ing = _____

    c) terrible + ly = _____

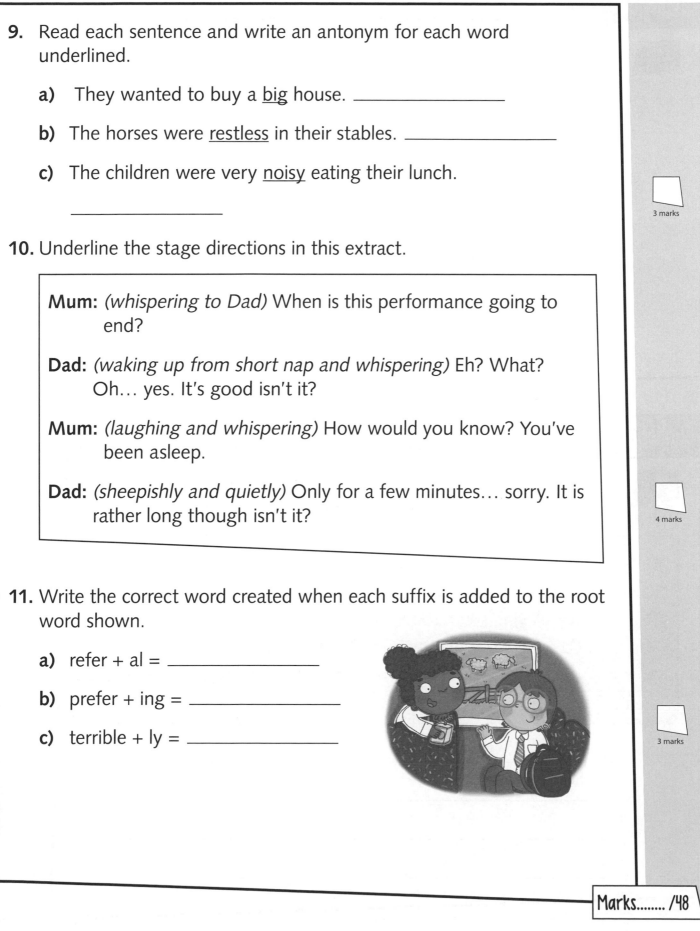

3 marks

Marks........ /48

Formal Speech and Writing

G Grammar   P Punctuation   S Spelling

Challenge 1

G **1** Write **F** next to the writing that would need to be formal and **I** next to the writing that would need to be informal.

a) a postcard to a friend

b) a letter of complaint

c) a conversation between friends in a story

d) a note from your mum to a teacher

e) a note to a friend

f) a report about an incident

6 marks

Marks.......... /6

Challenge 2

1 This conversation is written in informal language. Rewrite the conversation using formal language.

"Hiya, how ya' doing?" asked Glen.
"Hiya mate, I'm doing good!" replied Sam.
"Do ya' fancy playing some footie later?" asked Glen.
"Yeah, that'd be awesome! What time?" asked Sam.
"Anytime you feel like coming down, I'll be there 'bout six," replied Glen.
'Great, see ya' there!"

_____

_____

_____

_____

6 marks

Marks.......... /6

Formal Speech and Writing

Challenge 3

1 When writing formally you should **not** use personal pronouns to refer to yourself or the reader. Read the passage below and underline the personal pronouns.

> I think that we should not have to wear our coats at school if we do not want to. We know whether we are cold so no one can tell us how we are feeling. Our opinion should be taken into account, don't you think?

10 marks

2 Rewrite the passage above so that it does not contain personal pronouns or phrases that show a personal opinion. You can add details if you wish to.

_____

_____

_____

_____

_____

3 marks

Marks......... /13

Total marks .... /25   How am I doing?   😊   😐   😣

Different Verbs

G Grammar   P Punctuation   S Spelling

Challenge 1

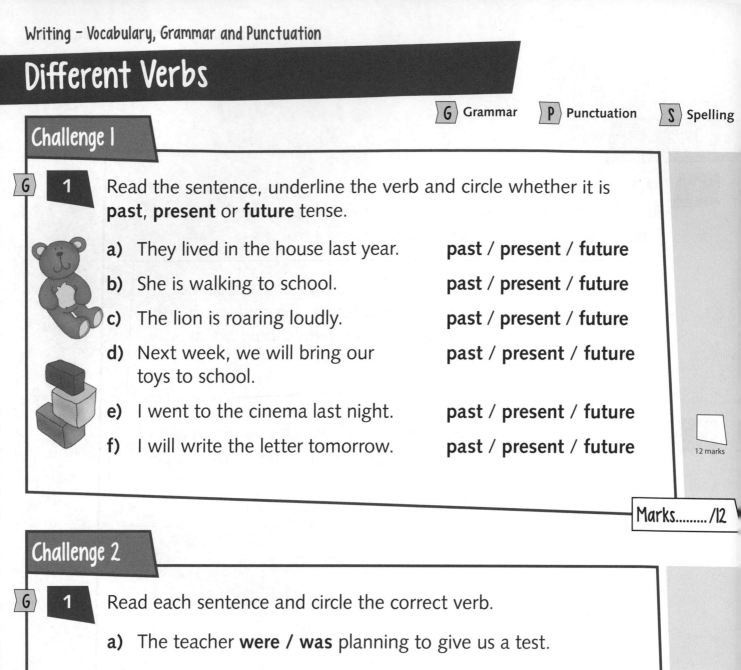

G **1** Read the sentence, underline the verb and circle whether it is **past**, **present** or **future** tense.

a) They lived in the house last year.   **past / present / future**

b) She is walking to school.   **past / present / future**

c) The lion is roaring loudly.   **past / present / future**

d) Next week, we will bring our toys to school.   **past / present / future**

e) I went to the cinema last night.   **past / present / future**

f) I will write the letter tomorrow.   **past / present / future**

12 marks

Marks........ /12

Challenge 2

G **1** Read each sentence and circle the correct verb.

a) The teacher **were / was** planning to give us a test.

b) I watched carefully and **wonder / wondered** what the magician was going to pull from his hat.

c) The animals **has / have** lots of places to sit in the shade.

d) The Queen **was opening / opened** the new building when she fell over.

e) The cinema **is / are** open today.

f) The computer **works / worked** yesterday.

6 marks

Different Verbs

2 Complete each sentence using the verbs below.

| watched | made | is | helped |

a) They _____ to bake the cakes for the sale.

b) The children _____ a mess.

c) The school _____ closed today because of snow.

d) The parents _____ the school play yesterday.

4 marks

Marks......... /10

Challenge 3

1 Underline the **modal** verb in each sentence.

a) We could go swimming today.

b) The children mustn't go onto the grass.

c) We must eat healthy food.

d) The teacher agreed that they could go on the climbing frame.

e) I can do anything I choose!

5 marks

2 Write a modal verb to complete each sentence to show **certainty**.

a) It is snowing so we _____ wear our coats outside.

b) The computer was broken so they _____ use it.

c) We _____ eat lunch as the food is not ready.

d) She asked if she _____ go to the toilet.

e) We _____ go out to play as the sun is shining.

5 marks

Marks......... /10

Total marks .... /32   How am I doing?   😊 😐 😣

Adverbs

G) Grammar   P) Punctuation   S) Spelling

Challenge 1

G **1** Write each of the adverbs below in the correct column of the table to show whether it gives information about **when**, **where** or **how**.

yesterday | later | nearby | today | cheerfully

quietly | slowly | urgently | here | often | outside

tomorrow | now | there | kindly | everywhere

When	Where	How

16 marks

Marks......... /16

Challenge 2

G **1** Read the passage and underline the adverbs.

I walked quickly to the shop as it often closed at lunchtime. I had been caught out yesterday as it was closed when I arrived. Luckily, it was open today and I bought my shopping. I happily waved goodbye to the shopkeeper and strolled lazily home.

7 marks

Marks......... /7

Adverbs

Challenge 3

1 Fill in the missing adverbs (some of which are also adjectives) in the spaces below.

Example: well, better, **best**

a) bad, _____, worst   **b)** much, _____, most

c) little, less, _____   **d)** early, earlier, _____

4 marks

2 Use the adverbs you have written in question 1 above in the correct spaces to complete each of these sentences correctly.

Example: The game he liked **best** was cricket.

a) Getting things right is _____ important than finishing first.

b) Our team played _____ in the rain today.

c) He was the _____ one to arrive.

d) My favourite story is the one we have read the _____.

4 marks

3 Write a sentence containing each adverb shown below.

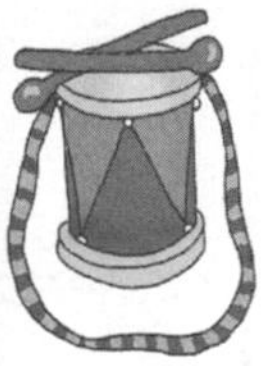

a) angrily _____

_____

b) sharply _____

_____

c) furthest _____

_____

3 marks

Marks.......... /11

Total marks .... /34   How am I doing?

Noun Phrases

G Grammar   P Punctuation   S Spelling

Challenge 1

G **1** Underline the **expanded noun phrases** used in each sentence.

   a) The young man walked to school.

   b) An old lady with a stick chased the dog away.

   c) Yellow meadow butterflies need to be protected.

   d) I walked towards the sandy beach.

   e) He was wearing a nice blue shirt.

   f) The swimming pool in town is new.

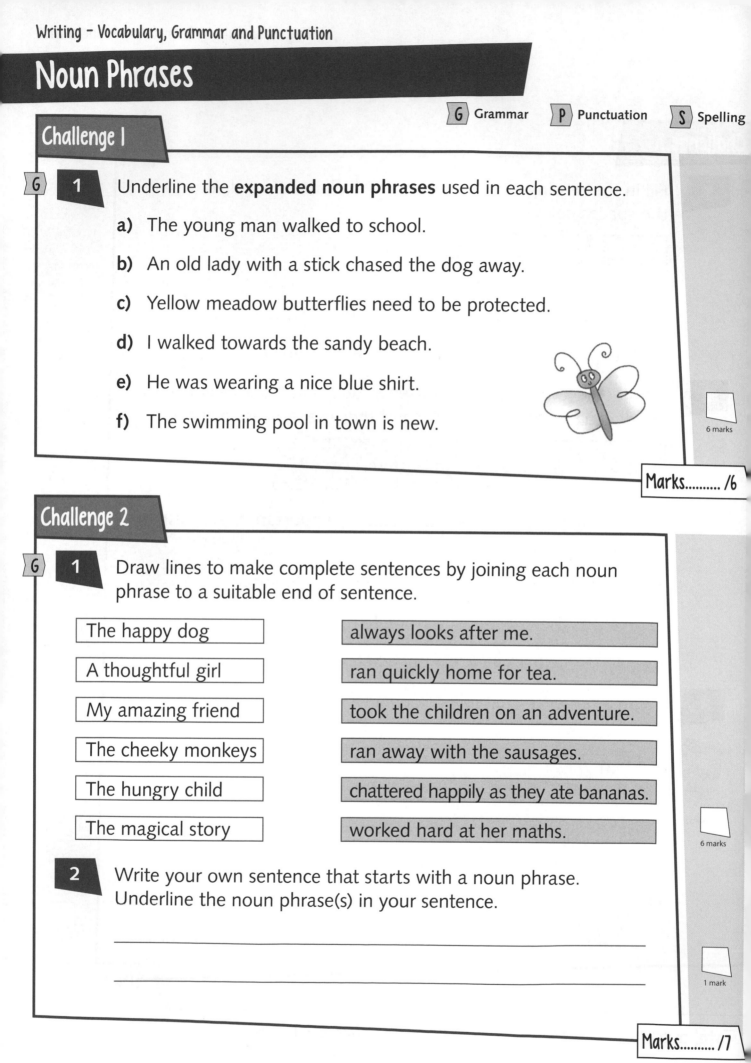

6 marks

Marks.......... /6

Challenge 2

G **1** Draw lines to make complete sentences by joining each noun phrase to a suitable end of sentence.

The happy dog	always looks after me.
The magical story	ran quickly home for tea.
My amazing friend	took the children on an adventure.
The cheeky monkeys	ran away with the sausages.
The hungry child	chattered happily as they ate bananas.
The magical story	worked hard at her maths.

6 marks

2 Write your own sentence that starts with a noun phrase. Underline the noun phrase(s) in your sentence.

_____

_____

1 mark

Marks.......... /7

Noun Phrases

1 For each noun phrase, rewrite it so that it has the opposite meaning.

Example: The friendly cat **The unfriendly cat**

a) The unhelpful man _____

b) The happy swarm of bees _____

c) My old car _____

d) The useful bicycle _____

4 marks

2 Insert each noun phrase that you wrote in question 1 above (including the example given) into the correct sentence below.

a) _____ chased after

and stung the herd of antelope.

b) I went to the tip and threw away

_____.

c) I was scratched by

_____.

d) _____ helped the old

lady onto the bus.

e) I was excited to drive away in

_____.

5 marks

Marks.........../9

Total marks ..../22   How am I doing? 😊 😐 😣

93

Verb Prefixes

Challenge 1

SG **1** Choose the correct prefix to place in front of each verb in these sentences.

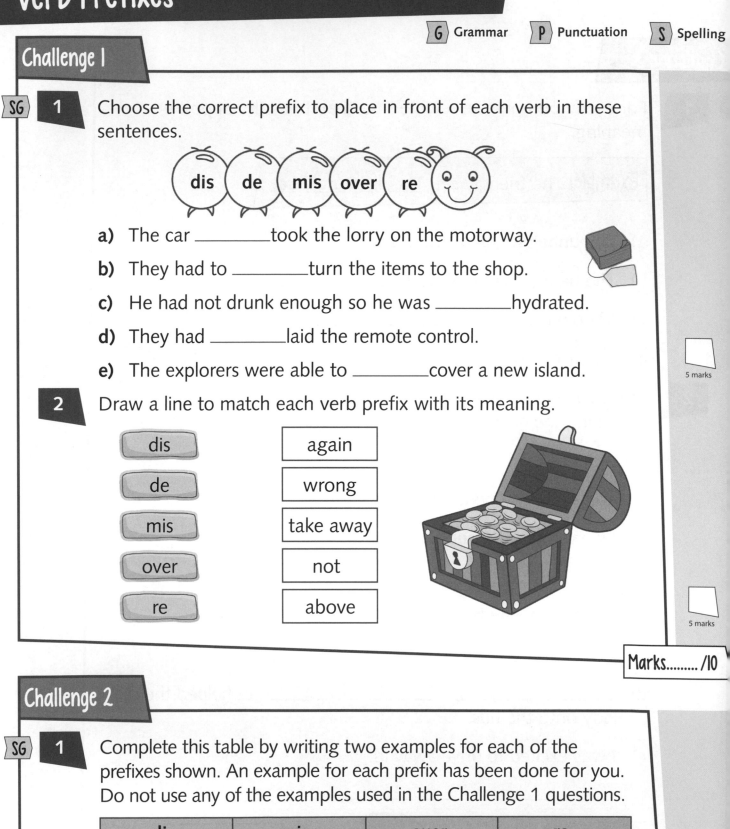

dis   de   mis   over   re

a) The car _____took the lorry on the motorway.

b) They had to _____turn the items to the shop.

c) He had not drunk enough so he was _____hydrated.

d) They had _____laid the remote control.

e) The explorers were able to _____cover a new island.

5 marks

2 Draw a line to match each verb prefix with its meaning.

dis	again
de	wrong
mis	take away
over	not
re	above

5 marks

Marks......... /10

Challenge 2

SG **1** Complete this table by writing two examples for each of the prefixes shown. An example for each prefix has been done for you. Do not use any of the examples used in the Challenge 1 questions.

dis-	mis-	over-	re-
disrespect	*mishear*	*overtake*	*retake*

8 marks

Marks.......... /8

Verb Prefixes

Challenge 3

1 Complete each sentence by adding the correct verb prefix so that it makes sense.

a) I had to _____ do my work because it was incorrect.

b) The robot was able to _____ fuse the bomb.

c) The phone was _____ connected from the socket.

d) The boy _____ reacted to the football tackle.

e) They had to _____ call the chocolate as it had been made wrongly.

f) The children were _____ appointed that sports day was cancelled.

g) Sam _____ understood the instruction.

7 marks

2 Read the passage and insert the correct words so that it makes sense. Then underline the words that are verbs.

| mistake | disobedient | remark | overflow | misbehaved |

Boris was a very _____ boy and often

_____. People would _____ on his

bad behaviour. One day he made a big _____

as he allowed the bath he was filling to _____;

there was water everywhere!

12 marks

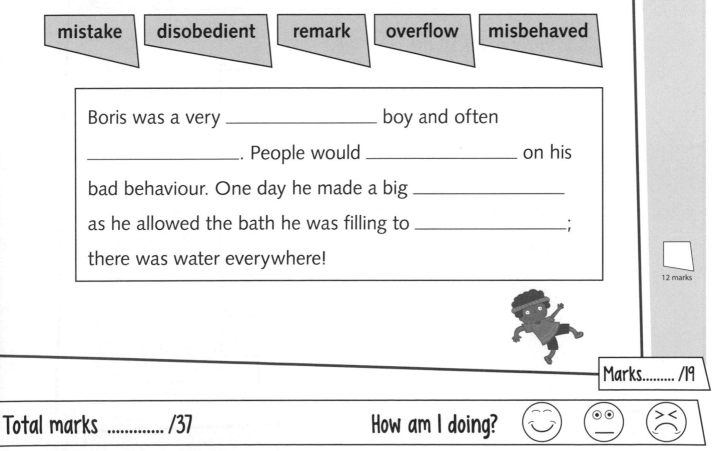

Marks........ /19

Total marks .... /37   How am I doing? 😊 😐 😣

Different Sentences

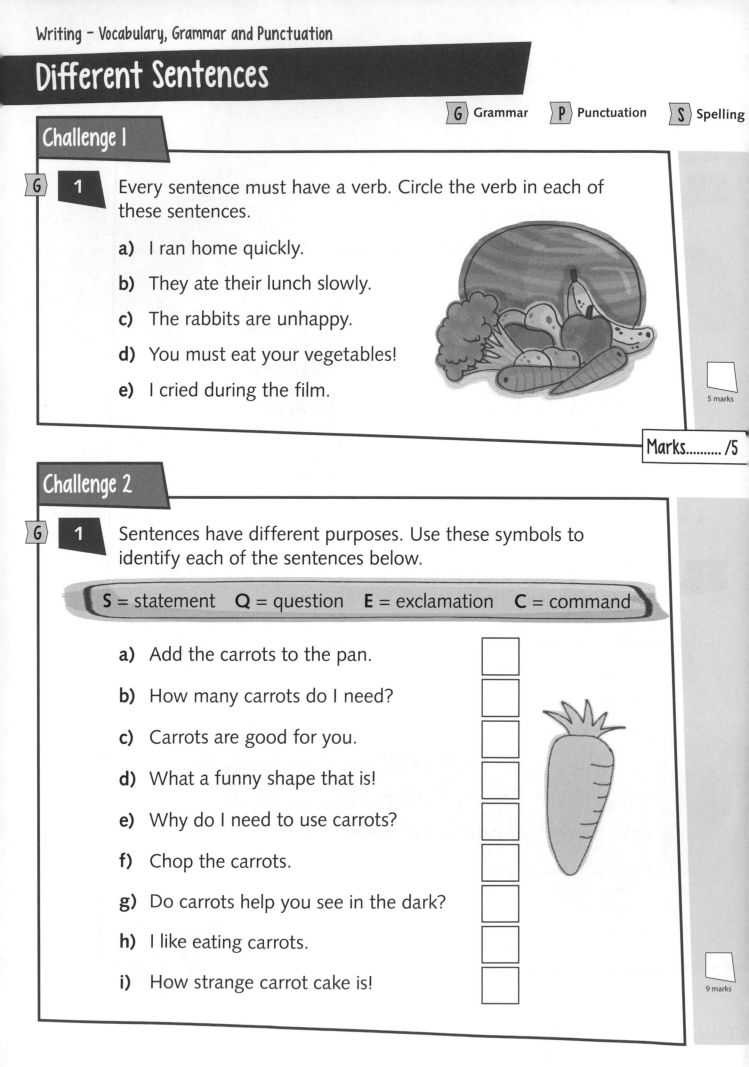

G Grammar   **P** Punctuation   **S** Spelling

Challenge 1

G 1 Every sentence must have a verb. Circle the verb in each of these sentences.

a) I ran home quickly.

b) They ate their lunch slowly.

c) The rabbits are unhappy.

d) You must eat your vegetables!

e) I cried during the film.

5 marks

Marks.......... /5

Challenge 2

G 1 Sentences have different purposes. Use these symbols to identify each of the sentences below.

S = statement   **Q** = question   **E** = exclamation   **C** = command

a) Add the carrots to the pan.

b) How many carrots do I need?

c) Carrots are good for you.

d) What a funny shape that is!

e) Why do I need to use carrots?

f) Chop the carrots.

g) Do carrots help you see in the dark?

h) I like eating carrots.

i) How strange carrot cake is!

9 marks

Different Sentences

2 Write your own sentences about your favourite hobby.

a) question _____

b) exclamation _____

c) statement _____

d) command _____

4 marks

Marks......... /13

Challenge 3

1 Write whether each sentence has **1** or **2** clauses.

a) The cat is wet. ☐

b) I really like to eat lots of tasty vegetables. ☐

c) I walked home because it was dry. ☐

d) I ate lunch but I didn't have dessert. ☐

e) Cats do not like the rain. ☐

f) Fish like water, but cats do not like water. ☐

6 marks

2 Circle the conjunction in each of these sentences.

a) Lizzie went to Freya's house and played games with her.

b) Chan likes rugby but Jennifer prefers tennis.

c) Coby was upset as he had lost his rabbit.

d) Unless you work hard you will not improve.

e) However much you cry, you will still not have any sweets!

5 marks

Marks......... /11

Total marks .... /29   How am I doing? ☺ 😐 😣

Relative Clauses

Challenge 1

G **1** Circle the **relative pronoun** in each of these sentences.

a) This is the table that everyone is admiring.

b) I have a cat whose hair keeps falling out.

c) Rosie is happy now that her skipping rope has been found.

d) James, whom I think is funny, is my friend.

e) The laptop, that I was using at the time, broke.

f) The bike which I ride is very new.

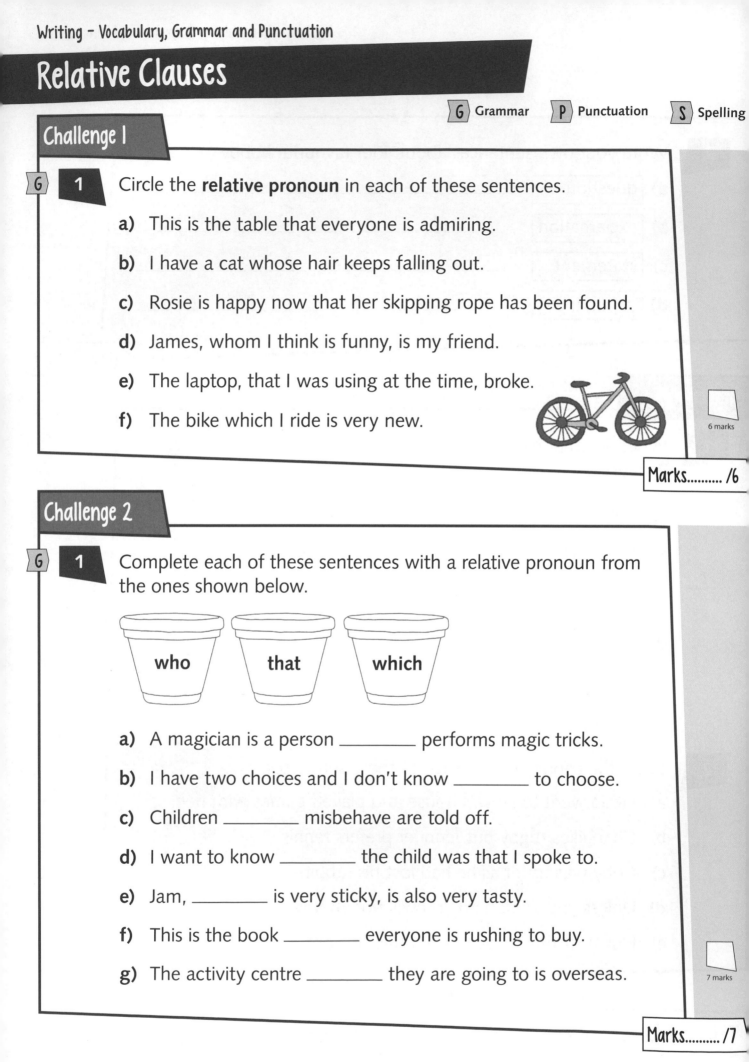

6 marks

Marks.......... /6

Challenge 2

G **1** Complete each of these sentences with a relative pronoun from the ones shown below.

who   that   which

a) A magician is a person _____ performs magic tricks.

b) I have two choices and I don't know _____ to choose.

c) Children _____ misbehave are told off.

d) I want to know _____ the child was that I spoke to.

e) Jam, _____ is very sticky, is also very tasty.

f) This is the book _____ everyone is rushing to buy.

g) The activity centre _____ they are going to is overseas.

7 marks

Marks.......... /7

Relative Clauses

Challenge 3

1 Choose from the words in bold to write the correct relative pronouns in the sentences.

a) I need someone _____ (**who** / **whose**) can look after my rabbits.

b) I will take you to a shop _____ (**who** / **which**) sells amazing sweets.

c) Where did you buy the necklace _____ (**who** / **that**) you wore last week?

d) I have a brother _____ (**who** / **whose**) is exceptional at tennis.

e) His mum, _____ (**whom** / **which**) he saw yesterday, gave him a huge hug.

f) I have a friend _____ (**whom** / **whose**) jewellery is very beautiful.

g) _____ (**Whichever** / **Whoever**) choice you make, you will upset someone!

h) Granny knits cardigans _____ (**whom** / **which**) are always beautiful.

i) We don't know the boy _____ (**who** / **whose**) fell out of the tree.

9 marks

Marks.......... /9

Total marks .... /22   How am I doing?   😊 😐 😣

Tense Choices

G Grammar   **P** Punctuation   **S** Spelling

Challenge 1

G **1** Write **P** (past) or **F** (future) by each sentence to show which tense it is written in.

a) The monkey fell off the branch. ☐

b) The boys will play football. ☐

c) The driver will have an accident. ☐

d) Sam injured his leg last week. ☐

e) The children completed the challenge. ☐

f) The swimmer is going to compete in a race. ☐

6 marks

Marks.......... /6

Challenge 2

G **1** Circle the correct form of the verb to complete each sentence.

a) We (**have** / **had**) to work hard to finish the test yesterday.

b) They (**ran** / **run**) very fast in last week's race.

c) Chris (**ate** / **eats**) his lunch very fast so he could play football.

d) The giraffe will (**come** / **came**) out of his house soon.

e) The playground (**is** / **are**) open today.

f) When (**would** / **will**) the sun come out?

g) He (**has** / **have**) worked hard to win that medal.

h) The museum (**is** / **was**) interesting when they visited it.

i) She (**want** / **wanted**) everyone to (**come** / **came**) to her party.

9 marks

Marks.......... /9

Tense Choices

Challenge 3

1 Complete the table to show what the verb '**to be**' is in the present and past tenses.

Subject	Past Tense	Present Tense
I	**a)**	am
you	were	**b)**
he / she / it	was	**c)**
we	**d)**	are
they	**e)**	**f)**

6 marks

2 Complete each sentence using the correct verb form of the verb '**to be**'.

a) I _____ very late to school yesterday.

b) It _____ now time to leave.

c) They _____ in a lot of trouble last week.

d) She _____ walking very fast along the road ahead of us.

e) I _____ learning to ride my bike today.

f) We _____ excited to see land ahead.

6 marks

Marks.........../12

Total marks ..../27   How am I doing?

Adverbials of Time, Place and Number

 **G** Grammar 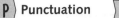 **P** Punctuation **S** Spelling

Challenge 1

G **1** Underline the adverbial phrase in each sentence.

a) She drove the car as fast as possible.

b) The carpenter hit the nail with a hammer.

c) As quickly as possible, I sold the strange beads.

d) The aeroplane flew swiftly through the cloud.

e) The children walked in silence.

f) The adventurers set off over the mountain.

g) I went to watch the football later than planned.

h) The wolves were howling loudly nearby.

i) Firstly, I want to thank your parents.

9 marks

Marks.......... /9

Challenge 2

G **1** For each of the adverbs / adverbial phrases below, write whether it gives information about **T** (time), **P** (place) or **N** (number).

a) later that night ☐

b) finally ☐

c) near the woods ☐

d) over in the trees ☐

e) early that morning ☐

f) after the games ☐

g) out of the building ☐

h) secondly ☐

8 marks

Marks.......... /8

Adverbials of Time, Place and Number

1 Underline the adverbials in each sentence.
Then put a tick next to the sentences that have fronted adverbials.

a) Finally, the duck eggs arrived.

b) Later that morning, we all had a snack.

c) The parents were all waiting nearby to meet us.

d) Early last week, we left for our school trip.

e) My friend turned down the nearest road.

f) Ariel and the Prince had to kiss before sunset.

g) Whenever it is possible, I say thank you to my mum.

h) I saw lots of sweets in the window of the shop.

i) With a great deal of thought, he made his choice.

9 marks

2 For each adverbial above, write whether it gives information about **how**, **where** or **when** for the verb.

a) _____ b) _____

c) _____ d) _____

e) _____ f) _____

g) _____ h) _____

i) _____

9 marks

Marks.......... /18

Total marks .... /35   How am I doing?   😊 😐 😖

Commas for Meaning

G Grammar   P Punctuation   S Spelling

Challenge 1

P 1 Rewrite each sentence, adding commas to separate the items in the lists.

a) The kit list said I needed shorts t-shirts shoes socks pants and a warm jumper.

_____

_____

b) At school today, I have Maths English Science Geography and PE.

_____

_____

2 marks

Marks............/2

Challenge 2

P 1 Rewrite the sentences, adding commas to show parenthesis.

a) The girls who were called Freya and Eliza played in the playhouse.

_____

_____

b) The chicken coop which Harry's dad had built had been at school for years.

_____

_____

c) The nursery children who were all three or four years old couldn't wait to go to the zoo.

_____

_____

3 marks

Marks.........../3

Commas for Meaning

1 After a fronted adverbial there **must always** be a comma. Rewrite these sentences adding a comma after each fronted adverbial.

a) All day long the children worked.

_____

b) Behind the pond the frogs made their home.

_____

c) Under the sea the mermaids sang their songs.

_____

3 marks

2 For each sentence, write your own fronted adverbial and add the comma in the correct place.

> **Example:** He walked to the bus stop.
> <u>As quickly as he could,</u> he walked to the bus stop.

a) The children cheered. _____

_____

b) The dog escaped. _____

_____

c) The whale came up for air. _____

_____

6 marks

Marks.......... /9

Total marks .... /14   How am I doing?   😊   😐   😣

Brackets, Dashes and Commas

G Grammar   P Punctuation   S Spelling

Challenge 1

P 1 Rewrite the sentences inserting brackets to indicate parenthesis.

a) I have lots of hobbies karate, reading, fishing and playing football that I spend my free time doing.

_____

_____

b) I had lots of presents for my birthday money, clothes and cinema vouchers.

_____

_____

c) She answered the question after a long pause and got it correct.

_____

_____

3 marks

Marks........../3

Challenge 2

P 1 Rewrite these sentences, inserting double dashes to show parenthesis.

a) Last night, Jacob a security guard caught two men trying to break into the school.

_____

_____

b) The car that was travelling very slowly held up all the traffic.

_____

_____

2 marks

Marks........../2

Brackets, Dashes and Commas

Challenge 3

1 Some of these sentences are punctuated incorrectly. Put a cross at the end of the incorrect sentences and a tick at the end of the correct ones.

a) Aisha (my best friend) came over to play. ☐

b) Mrs Thompson (my piano teacher inspired me) so much. ☐

c) The weather was lovely beautiful, actually so we went to the beach. ☐

d) The children all from – Class 5 – did not do as they were told. ☐

e) Samuel a, thoughtful boy, liked to sit quietly and think. ☐

5 marks

2 For the sentences that you have marked as incorrect, rewrite them on the lines below using the correct punctuation.

_____

_____

_____

_____

_____

_____

_____

_____

4 marks

Marks.......... /9

Total marks .... /14   How am I doing? 😊 😐 😣

Progress Test 4

G **1.** Tick the types of writing that would need to be written formally.

     a) newspaper report ☐

     b) postcard to a friend ☐

     c) letter of apology to your teacher ☐

2 marks

G **2.** Read the sentence, underline the verb and circle whether it is **past, present** or **future** tense.

     a) She ran to school today.   **past / present / future**

     b) He will kick the football.   **past / present / future**

     c) They talked too much yesterday.   **past / present / future**

     d) You are beautiful.   **past / present / future**

4 marks

G **3.** Read each sentence and circle the correct **verb**.

     a) You **is / are** going to learn your times tables.

     b) They **built / build** a whole block of flats last year.

     c) I **have / has** lots of clothes to sell.

3 marks

G **4.** Underline the **adverbs** and **adverbials** in the sentences below.

     a) They listened carefully to the music.

     b) I hit the ball very hard.

     c) Last week, I ran a marathon.

     d) They crept quietly through the tunnel.

4 marks

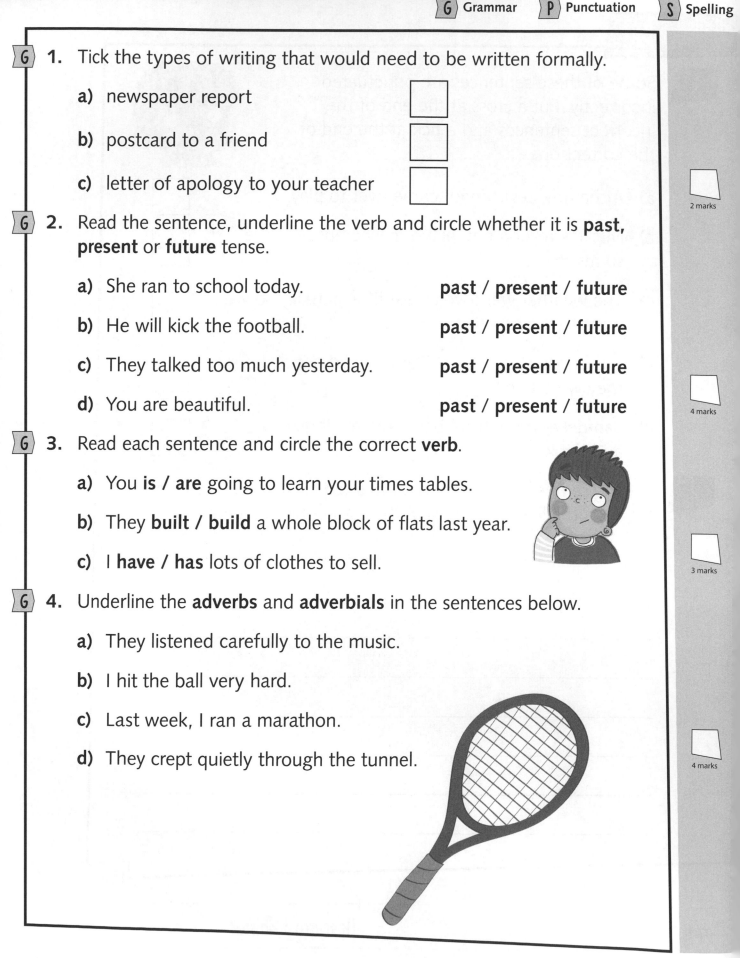

5. Underline the expanded noun phrase used in each sentence.

    a) The green crocodile ate his lunch.

    b) The old armchair with a broken cover was thrown on the tip.

    c) It was lovely to see the beautiful wildlife.

3 marks

6. Put the correct prefix in front of the words in these sentences.
Use the prefixes shown below.

    dis   **up**   **re**

    a) I had to _____verse down the lane.

    b) The accusation _____set her.

    c) I was _____tracted by the television.

3 marks

7. Add a suitable conjunction to each sentence.

    a) It is raining _____ the children had to stay inside.

    b) My friend likes broccoli _____ I like carrots.

    c) Samuel was sad _____ he had lost his favourite toy.

    d) _____ you do revision you will not do well in the test.

4 marks

8. Use these symbols to identify each of the sentences below.

S = statement   **Q** = question   **E** = exclamation   **C** = command

    a) How much do these cost?

    b) How strange that they are so expensive!

    c) Money doesn't grow on trees.

    d) Earn some more money.

4 marks

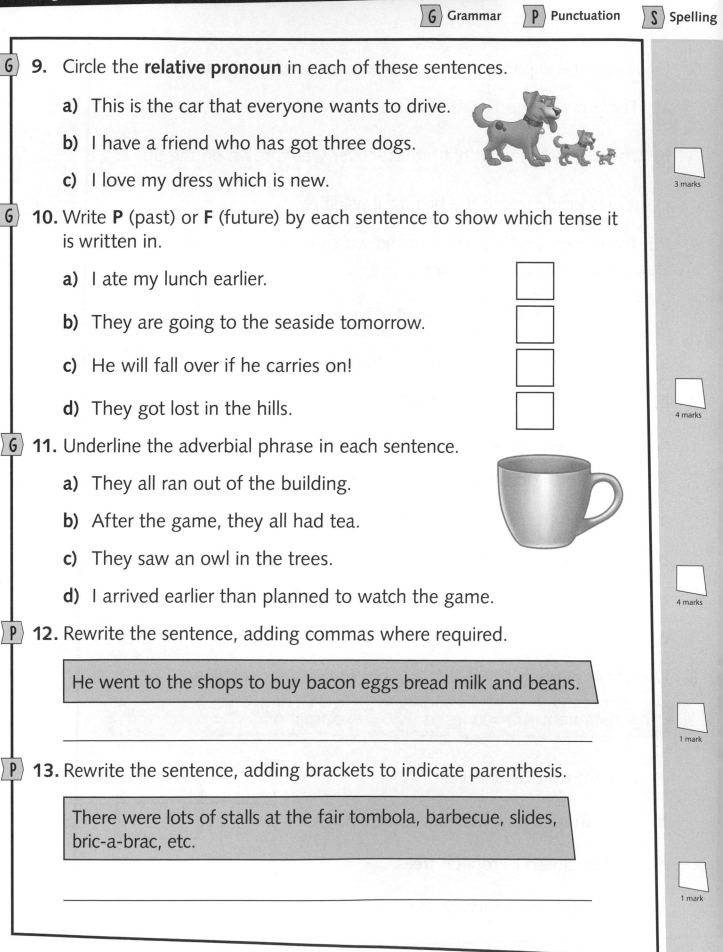

G **9.** Circle the **relative pronoun** in each of these sentences.

  a) This is the car that everyone wants to drive.

  b) I have a friend who has got three dogs.

  c) I love my dress which is new.

3 marks

G **10.** Write **P** (past) or **F** (future) by each sentence to show which tense it is written in.

  a) I ate my lunch earlier.

  b) They are going to the seaside tomorrow.

  c) He will fall over if he carries on!

  d) They got lost in the hills.

4 marks

G **11.** Underline the adverbial phrase in each sentence.

  a) They all ran out of the building.

  b) After the game, they all had tea.

  c) They saw an owl in the trees.

  d) I arrived earlier than planned to watch the game.

4 marks

P **12.** Rewrite the sentence, adding commas where required.

He went to the shops to buy bacon eggs bread milk and beans.

_____

1 mark

P **13.** Rewrite the sentence, adding brackets to indicate parenthesis.

There were lots of stalls at the fair tombola, barbecue, slides, bric-a-brac, etc.

_____

1 mark

14. Put a tick next to the sentence that is punctuated correctly.

A   James (my next-door) neighbour came to play with me. ☐

B   James (my next-door neighbour) came to play with me. ☐

C   James my (next-door neighbour) came to play with me. ☐

D   James my next-door (neighbour) came to play with me. ☐

1 mark

15. Draw lines to match the prefixes to their meanings.

auto		above / over
tele		again / beyond
super		self
re		far / far off

4 marks

16. Write **F** by the facts and **O** by the opinions.

a) Bats hang upside down. ☐

b) Bats are scary. ☐

c) Bats eat fruit. ☐

d) Bats are not liked by humans. ☐

4 marks

17. In each sentence, underline the homophone that has been used incorrectly. Write the correct homophone above each underlined word.

a) It was early in the mourning before the sun had risen.

b) They had to altar the dress to make it fit.

c) The cars were stationery on the motorway.

3 marks

18. Rewrite this dialogue with the correct punctuation.

Come and line up called the teacher

_____

1 mark

Marks........./52

Notes

Pages 4–11
Starter Test
1. a) **T**he children met at the entrance to the zoo**.**
    b) **H**ave you lost your car keys**?**
    c) **W**hat big ears you have**, G**randma**!**
    d) **I** need to catch the bus home**.**
2. b) "Please can you help me?" asked Peter. ✓
3. a) lions   b) foxes   c) snails
    d) zoos   e) heroes   f) halves
    g) babies   h) sheep
4. a) The **kind** girl helped the **sad** boy.
    b) The **smelly** warthog was friends with the **excitable** meerkat.
    c) The **dusty** book lay on the **old, wooden** shelf.
5. a) He **is** a fast runner.
    b) They **are** not friends.
    c) Siobhan **ate** her dinner quickly.
6. a) I like sailing **and** I like swimming.
    b) We had to go in **because** it was snowing!
    c) I am a fast runner **but** I do not like running!
7. b) Are you still poorly? ✓
8. Sebastian, Christmas, Germany, June, Monday
9. Before we left**,** the children checked their luggage.
10. a) What a strange day it has been! ✓
11. a) helped   b) flew   c) gave
12. a) **re/uni**cycle b) **un**fair   c) **dis**obey
13. a) He gent**ly** placed the baby in the cot.
    b) There was a huge amount of excite**ment** about the party.
    c) Jake is tall**er** than Owen.
    d) The spring in the launchpad is very power**ful**.
14. a) "I am not happy about this," said the teacher.
    b) Chan whispered, "I am very bored!"
15. a) The children hid **behind** the door.
    b) The pirates climbed **up** the ladder.
    c) Mermaids live **under** the sea.
16. Answers will vary, e.g.
    a) The children ran **quickly / slowly** up the hill.
    b) The crowd cheered **loudly** for the actors.
    c) Children were playing **happily** in the playground.
17. a) There are over 5,000 different species of frog in the world.
    b) Most frogs start their lives as frogspawn.
    c) Frogs that are born as 'full frogs' can live far away from water.
    d) Frogs do not need to drink water as they absorb it through their skin.
    e) **Any two from:** insects, earthworms, minnows, spiders.
18. a) decide   b) position   c) notice
    d) fruit   e) group   f) guard
    g) build   h) arrive
19. a) don't   b) can't
    c) won't   d) I'll
20. a) **a** cup   b) **an** elephant c) **an** alien
    d) **a** phone   e) **a** friend   f) **a** yacht
21. <u>Before he could leave the house</u>, James had to unlock the front door.
22. a) Robot X953-7
    b) homework
    c) It can read a book and summarise it so you don't have to read it.
    d) Answers will vary, e.g. It costs £79.99
    e) It is truly amazing!
23. a) persuasion **b)** report   **c)** description

Pages 12–13
Challenge 1
1. a) test   b) try   c) like
    d) care   e) rely
Challenge 2
1.

foot	chair	**football**
light	ball	**lighthouse**
arm	bow	**armchair**
pan	house	**pancake**
rain	cake	**rainbow**

Challenge 3
1. Answers will vary, e.g.
    a) assistant / assistance / assisting
    b) recover / covering / uncover
    c) lightning / relight / enlighten / lighter
    d) report / portable / support
    e) approval / proving / disapprove
2. a) time   b) earth
    c) empty   d) carry

Pages 14–15
Challenge 1
1. a) mistake   b) submarine
    c) preview   d) disrespect
    e) unhurt

Answers

2.

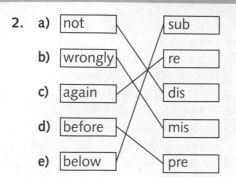

a) not — mis
b) wrongly — dis
c) again — re
d) before — pre
e) below — sub

Challenge 2
1.
a) The magician made the rabbit dis**appear**.
b) They had to un**cover** the truth.
c) The recipe said to pre**heat** the oven at the start.
d) They had to sub**merge** the object in water.

Challenge 3
1.
a) **un**comfortable   b) **re**written
c) **pre**caution   d) **re**turn
e) **un**tied   f) **mis**behave
g) **re**do

2.
a) **super**natural – not natural
b) **micro**scope – something used for viewing very small objects
c) **sub**heading – a title given to a small section of writing
d) **re**appear – appear again
e) **in**active – not involving physical activity

Pages 16–17
Challenge 1
1.
a) proud**est**   b) child**ish**   c) glad**ly**
d) care**ful**   e) cold**er**   f) help**less**
g) excite**ment**   h) kind**ness**

Challenge 2
1.
a) ador**able**   b) vaca**tion**
c) educa**tion**   d) desir**able**
e) agree**able**   f) attrac**tion**

2. Our new kitten is **adorable**.

Challenge 3
1.
a) The situation was **hopeless** as the car was stuck in the sand.
b) The football team held a **celebration** when they won the cup final.
c) The child was **thoughtful** as he stared at the page of questions.
d) When she won the competition it was the **greatest** day of her life!
e) **Sadly**, some animals are becoming extinct.
f) He gave an **explanation** of what he had found out from his research.
g) Superman liked to show off his **greatness** whenever he had the chance!

h) It is usually **warmer** in Spain than it is in England.

2. Answers will vary, e.g.
a) I **quietly / quickly / happily** walked to school.
b) It was the **greatest / saddest / happiest** day of my week.
c) He was **sitting / jumping / climbing** on a chair.
d) The child was **wondering / thinking / planning** what to do next.

Pages 18–19
Challenge 1
1.
a) James had to **re**turn the bike because it was broken.
b) The children used a **micro**scope to view the insects clearly.
c) The journalist made a **mis**take in the newspaper report.
d) The magician made the rabbit **dis**appear / **re**appear.
e) It was **im**possible for them to win the race now.
f) The pea under the mattress made the bed **un**comfortable.

Challenge 2
1.
a) They were a music**al** family as they all played instruments.
b) There was great excite**ment** when he won the race.
c) The children were very friend**ly** to the new child in the class.
d) The shoes were very comfort**able**.
e) The children had fun jump**ing** into the swimming pool.
f) The cheetah is the fast**est** land mammal.

Challenge 3
1.
a) They used a refer**ence** book to find the answer to their question.
b) He prefer**red** to eat jam rather than marmite on his toast.
c) There was a lot of cough**ing** in assembly this morning!
d) The band merr**ily** played their tunes.
e) I am happ**ier** in the summer than in the winter!
f) It was the sad**dest** I had ever felt.
g) The radio was port**able** so I took it into the garden.
h) The monkeys cheek**ily** stole the man's hat!
i) I had to be very sens**ible** when I crossed the road.

2. Answers will vary, e.g.
   a) The children were **astonished / surprised / excited** to find treasure at the end of the rainbow.
   b) We had a very **uncomfortable / restless** night because it was so hot.

Pages 20–21
Challenge 1
1. a) Sam was <u>allowed</u> to go to the park.
   b) They put the <u>bridle</u> on the horse.
   c) I had some <u>cereal</u> for breakfast this morning.
   d) After the main course, we had some <u>dessert</u>.
   e) I had to <u>draft</u> my work before I wrote it neatly.
   f) I <u>guessed</u> the answer correctly.
   g) We walked <u>past</u> the swimming pool on our way to school.
   h) I saw a <u>herd</u> of cows from my car window.
Challenge 2
1. a) The **knight** rode bravely on his horse.
   b) The man **led** the horse along the beach.
   c) Her **father** picked her up from school.
   d) They made their **descent** down the mountain.
   e) The teacher gave the child a good piece of **advice**.
2. Answers will vary, e.g.
   a) They sailed to the sandy **isle**.
   b) She walked down the **aisle** of the church.
Challenge 3
1. a) bee   b) witch   c) floor
   d) caught; seen   e) guest; father
   f) band; allowed; morning
2. a) She bought a new mobile **device** with her pocket money.
   b) They went to netball **practice** after school.
   c) "**Who's** been eating my porridge?"

Pages 22–23

Challenge 1
1.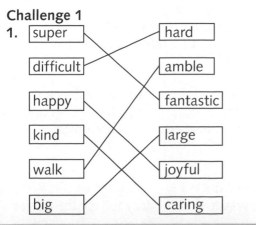

Challenge 2
1. a) noisy   b) under   c) far
   d) after   e) correct   f) cold
2. a) dirty   b) quiet   c) easy
Challenge 3
1. a) The school day was **over**.
   b) The young **man** looked smart in his suit.
   c) Most of the answers were **wrong**.
   d) They all looked **alike** in their school uniform.
   e) The shop was very **close** to their house.
2. Answers will vary, e.g.

Word	Synonym	Antonym
rich	wealthy	poor
young	youthful	old
expensive	luxurious / costly	cheap
stop	halt	go / start

Pages 24–25
Challenge 1
1. a) advert   b) **6** hours
   c) **Any two from**: tractor ride / listen to music / watch tractor demonstrations / sheep-shearing
   d) to persuade
Challenge 2
1. a) recount   b) description   c) persuasion
Challenge 3
1. a) newspaper
   b) diary
   c) poetry
   d) biography (also accept newspaper)

Pages 26–27
Challenge 1
1. newspaper – written in columns
   recipe – numbered steps
   story – beginning, middle and end
   advert – slogans
Challenge 2
1. a) She had made them many times before.
   b) However, today was going to prove to be very different from the other times she had made them.
   c) **Any two from**: not loud / unusual / it came from the oven.
Challenge 3
1. a) recount
   b) title / paragraph explaining where they were going
   c) chronological order

Answers

Pages 28–29
Challenge 1

1.
fantasy	– imagined places and people – not based in reality
myth	– a traditional story involving supernatural beings and / or events
adventure	– the characters go somewhere exciting / dangerous / fun
mystery	– something has to be solved
science fiction	– ideas including space, time travel and the future

Challenge 2
1.

Mystery	Fairy Tale	Science Fiction
police station jewellery shop	magical castle forest little cottage	planets moon spaceships

Challenge 3
1. a) myth   b) mystery   c) horror
   d) science fiction   e) adventure

Pages 30–31
Challenge 1
1. a) letters   b) to inform
   c) parents   d) Text A

Challenge 2
1. a) inform   b) popped
   c) That Frankie will help himself / herself to snacks and drinks anyway.

Challenge 3
1. a) Text A
   b) Answers will vary, e.g. Words like 'luncheon' are not usually used today.
   c) awesome   d) Answers will vary.
   e) Answers will vary.

Pages 32–33
Challenge 1
1. Listen to the performance of your child. 1 mark for audibility, 1 mark for learning by heart, 1 mark for getting humour across.

Challenge 2
1. a) crocodile   b) Nile   c) No
   d) He is eating them.   e) 2   f) 4
   g) scale   h) ABAB

Challenge 3
1. a) d e f / i / n i t e / l y
   b) h e l p / l e s s / n e s s
   c) e l / e / p h a n t
   d) l i s t / e / n i n g

2. Cool / breeze,
   Spark / ling / wa / ter,
   Sun / bla / zing / on / my / back.
   Gol / den / sand / be / tween / my / warm / toes…
   the / beach.
3. Green / and / sca / led / legs,   5
   Squelch / ing / slow / ly / through / the / mud   7
   Watch / ing / for / its / prey.   5

Pages 34–35
Challenge 1
1.
Peter Pan	– fights a bad pirate
Goldilocks	– breaks into a house
The Gruffalo	– is scared of a mouse
Big Bad Wolf	– blows down houses

Challenge 2
1. a) She is too busy packing and they are not ready to leave.
   b) The dog has tripped him up and he has hurt his foot.
   c) She is not as scary as she seems: "her bark is worse than her bite".
   d) playing a game on his phone

Challenge 3
1. All stage directions (in italics) should be underlined. (1 mark for each)
2. a) To tell what is happening / To show how a character is speaking
   b) colon

Pages 36–37
Challenge 1
1. a) a pause during an activity
   b) separate into pieces

Challenge 2
1. a) countries
2. Answers will vary, e.g.
   a) We **talk** to our friends a lot.
   b) We listened to a **talk** about animals at the weekend.

Challenge 3
1. a) the train   b) as fast as a blink
   c) rain that is blowing sideways   d) he is collecting brambles

Pages 38–39
Challenge 1
1. a) sunny / hot
   b) She was feeling too lazy to pick the daisies.

Challenge 2

1. a) To catch up with the rabbit.
   b) went like the wind
   c) frustrated / worried

Challenge 3

1. a) the *Jolly Roger*
   b) entrance to the river
   c) No
   d) Answers will vary, e.g. 'cannibal of the seas' / 'horror of her name'

Pages 40–41
Challenge 1

1. Answers will vary, e.g. What does it feel like when you first take-off in the rocket?

Challenge 2

1. a) 44
   Answers to the rest of this challenge will vary, e.g.
   b) What is the name of your wife?
   c) What do you enjoy doing in your spare time?

Challenge 3

1. a) What is the International Space Station?
   b) When was the International Space Station first launched?
   c) How big is the Space Station?

2. a) 2
   b) 2nd November 2000
   c) 6
   d) Lots of countries helped to build it and people from different countries live on it.

Pages 42–43
Challenge 1

1. A summary is a **short** version of the **original** text. It is usually only a **paragraph** long. It picks out the **main** points only.

Challenge 2

1. a) waiting in a queue
   b) being late to pick up her children
   c) Answers will vary, e.g. "I am fed up with waiting in this queue and am worried that I will be late to pick up my children from school."

Challenge 3

1. a) Headteacher
   b) the fumes / the noise
   c) No
   d) 'continued lack of communication'

Pages 44–45
Challenge 1

1. a) Facts are **true** pieces of information.

   b) Opinions are based on **personal** thoughts and feelings.

Challenge 2

1.

Facts	Opinions
A, D, E, G, H, I,	B, C, F, J

Challenge 3

1. a) "This has been the greatest football season ever. **Leicester City are the champions!** They are also the best team in the world! **They will take part in a Victory Parade to show the cup to their supporters. The Premier League trophy is 104 cm high and weighs about 25 kg!** I think they might have tired arms after lifting it!"
   [facts are in bold, opinions are underlined]

2. a)–d) Children's own answers but check that they are facts and opinions as requested.

Pages 46–49
Progress Test 1

1. a) form   b) port
   c) scope   d) vision

2. Answers may vary, e.g.
   a) housefly b) butterfly c) cupboard
   d) buttercup e) household

3. a) **un**helpful b) **mis**heard c) **dis**trust

4. a) great**est** b) tick**lish** c) hope**fully**
   d) hope**less** e) great**ness** f) expect**ant**

5. a) How can you **misunderstand** such a clear instruction?
   b) He was **unkind** his friend.
   c) They had to **prevent** the accident from occurring.

6. a) They were sent back to **re**take their test.
   b) The parents were stuck in traffic and were **un**able to collect their children.
   c) The magician made the hat **dis / re** appear.
   d) They were **re**presenting their country at the Olympics.
   e) They travelled to the bottom of the ocean in a **sub**marine.

7. a) A **draught** was coming from under the door.
   b) They went to the **bridal** shop to buy a wedding dress.
   c) Camels are good at walking across the **desert**.
   d) They ate rhubard crumble for **dessert**.
   e) The bride walked joyfully down the **aisle**.

Answers

8.

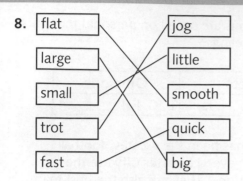

flat — quick
large — little
small — big
trot — smooth
fast — jog

9. Answers will vary, e.g.

Word	Synonym	Antonym
work	labour / job / slog	rest / play
open	ajar	closed / shut
tired	weary / sleepy	awake

10. a) science fiction **b)** adventure
c) mystery

11. a) They had separate entrances and separate playgrounds.
b) There was nothing on them.
c) Village schools had smaller numbers (but they still had larger classes than schools today).
d) slates
e) No – they had to copy or recite.
f) Children's own answer but must be backed up with examples from text.

Pages 50–51
Challenge 1
1. a) mistake **b)** preview **c)** distrust
d) retake **e)** unhurt
Challenge 2
1. a) **il**logical **b)** **in**active **c)** **ir**regular
d) **in**action **e)** **il**literate **f)** **in**capable
g) **in**visible **h)** **il**legal **i)** **ir**replaceable
Challenge 3
1.

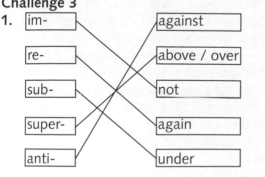

im- — not
re- — again
sub- — under
super- — above / over
anti- — against

2. a) We had to **sub**merge the sponge into the water.

b) It was **im**possible to see anything in the distance as it was so misty.
c) Thankfully, the mother was **re**united with her son after he had gone missing.
d) The children had a **super**natural experience when they pretended to visit aliens from another planet.
e) Sophie was given **anti**biotics when she went to the doctors.
f) The children were **re**turning from their trip late in the evening.
g) They managed to find the right **anti**dote to reverse the effect of the snake bite.
h) The **sub**title on the page explained what the paragraph was about.

Pages 52–53
Challenge 1
1. a) furniture **b)** happily **c)** gently
d) tension **e)** action
f) dangerous **g)** precious
Challenge 2
1. a) ✗ adoration **b)** ✗ admiration
c) ✓ **d)** ✗ causation
e) ✗ declaration **f)** ✓
Challenge 3
1. a) forgotten **b)** visited **c)** listening
d) preferred **e)** beginning **f)** travelling
2. a) referral **b)** transferring
c) transference **d)** offered
e) preferred

Pages 54–55
Challenge 1
1. a) i**s**land **b)** glis**t**en **c)** **w**rote
d) solem**n** **e)** **k**nock **f)** hym**n**
Challenge 2
1.

Silent t	Silent h	Silent k	Silent b	Silent d
Christmas	hour	knot	thumb	handsome
listen	white	knew	comb	badge
soften	ghost	knight	bomb	
fasten				

Challenge 3
1. a) climbed **b)** column **c)** build
d) crumbs **e)** castle **f)** school
g) guess **h)** sword **i)** autumn
j) rhinoceros

Pages 56–57
Challenge 1
1. a) The stars were shining in the dark **night**.

b) It was fun to **meet** my new baby sister.

c) I was allowed to **buy** some sweets at the shop.

d) There was **dew** on the grass in the morning.

e) The hotel **maid** tidied the room for us.

f) I found the book hard to **read**.

g) It was **their** turn to play on the climbing frame.

Challenge 2

1.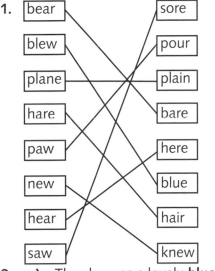

2. a) The sky was a lovely **blue** as the sun was shining.

   b) The dog had a thorn in its **paw**.

   c) I **saw** a **hare** running across the field.

   d) The grizzly **bear** was very scary!

Challenge 3

1. a) The bird **flew** away from the lady who was poorly with **flu**.

   b) A bee collects pollen from a **flower**. We use **flour** to bake cakes.

   c) It is **great** fun to **grate** cheese!

   d) We had an **hour** to complete **our** project.

   e) The bird **ate** the spider and all **eight** of its legs!

   f) I was proud when I **won one** medal at sports day.

   g) I work hard when I **write** because I want to get it **right**.

Pages 58–59
Challenge 1

1. a) My teacher gave me a good piece of **advice**.

   b) They had to **devise** a cunning plan to escape.

   c) I did lots of piano **practice** last night.

   d) We had to **proceed** with our plan.

e) Pens, pencils and scissors live in my **stationery** drawer.

Challenge 2

1. a) Can I ask **who's** responsible for finding out **whose** coat it is?

   b) You should be **wary** of lions when they are **weary** and wanting to sleep.

   c) My **father** ran **farther** than my mother.

   d) In the **past** year my brother **passed** his driving test.

   e) The **lead** on the roof **led** the thief to the building.

2. Children's own answers.

Challenge 3

1. I would <u>advice</u> you to listen carefully to the <u>advise</u> you are given about how a <u>guessed</u> must behave when at a hotel. My <u>farther</u> says that you must not wake up too early in the <u>mourning</u> and if you do you should be <u>quite</u>. If you have an electronic <u>devise</u> like an iPad then you should turn the volume down.

2. a) advise   b) advice   c) guest
   d) father   e) morning
   f) quiet   g) device

Pages 60–61
Challenge 1

1. a) ancient   b) bargain   c) familiar
   d) forty   e) occur   f) opportunity
   g) vegetable   h) vehicle

Challenge 2

1. bruise – an injury shown as discoloured skin

   dictionary – a book listing words / meanings of a language

   foreign – from a country different from your own

   neighbour – a person living next door or near

   soldier – a person who is in the army

Challenge 3

1. a) 2   b) 1   c) 3
2. Answers will vary, e.g.
   a) a group of people who govern a country
   b) a medium-sized sailing boat

Pages 62–63
Challenge 1

1. a) cheerful   b) content   c) happy
   d) jolly   e) joyful
   f) merry   g) pleased

Answers

Challenge 2

1. a) James **whispered** something quietly to Sam.
    b) They had to call for roadside **assistance**.
    c) She **thought** hard about the answer.
    d) I asked for some **help / support** to complete the work.

Challenge 3

1. a) It was a **rainy** day so all the animals were huddling for shelter.
    b) "Stop right there!" **shouted** the policeman.
    c) The money was **safe** as it was locked in the safe.
    d) I **jogged** to the shops to buy some sweets.
    e) The animals **stopped** when they saw the fire in the bushes.

2. The children **liked** Thursdays as it was the day they went **swimming.** They had to wear **sports** kit to school and take their swimming **kit** with them. The younger children swam in the **morning** and the **older** children swam in the afternoon. Lunch was always **delicious** too as it was roast dinner on a Thursday.

Pages 64–65
Challenge 1

1. a) rei**g**n   b) dou**b**t
    c) this**t**le   d) **k**night
    e) com**b**   f) hym**n**
    g) desi**g**n   h) **k**now

Challenge 2

1. a) ✓   b) ✓   c) ✓
    d) ✓   e) ✓   f) seize
    g) ✗ neither   h) ✗ weight

Challenge 3

1. a) I went to visit an **ancient** historical site yesterday.
    b) The **government** makes decisions about how our country is run.
    c) I had to **queue** for a long time at the ice-cream van.
    d) The teacher told us not to **interrupt** her when she was speaking.
    e) My swimming coach said I was doing **excellent** work in my training.
    f) We had a gymnastics **competition** at my club yesterday.
    g) I had the **opportunity** to go skiing with my class.
    h) The monkeys at the zoo were very **mischievous**.
    i) The lion was very **aggressive** when the meat was thrown into his cage.
    j) They could not **guarantee** that I would get a place on the skiing trip.
    k) The school hall could **accommodate** 450 people.
    l) The **committee** voted to buy new playground equipment for the school.

Pages 66–69
Progress Test 2

1. a) bargain   b) forty   c) harass
    d) temperature   e) curiosity
2. a) **in**take   b) **ir**regular
    c) **il**legal   d) **in**complete
3. a) ✗ profession   b) ✗ pronunciation
    c) ✓   d) ✗ observation   e) ✓
4. a) lam**b**   b) doub**t**   c) this**t**le
5. a) knew   b) sore   c) isle / I'll
6. a) I had to **alter** my design.
    b) They had to **bow** at the end of the play.
    c) A **prophet** is someone who foretells the future.
7. a) sacrifice   b) secretary   c) soldier
    d) suggest   e) symbol   f) system
8. a) It was a **chilly** day on Sunday so we all wore our coats.
    b) "I had a fantastic time today!" **bellowed** Freya.
    c) The **squad** played well during the match.
9. a) ✗ ancient   b) ✗ conscience
    c) ✓   d) ✗ sufficient   e) ✓
10. a) poetry   b) diary
11. writing
12. a) The excite**ment** was electric in the stadium.
    b) The rabbit had hurt his leg and lay help**less** in the field.
    c) They had to find a film suit**able** for children to watch.
    d) The children had to be sens**ible** in the line.
    e) They travel**led** a long way on the first day of the journey.
13. a) **in**complete b) **in**correct   c) **il**legible
    d) **in**definite   e) **ir**relevant

Pages 70–71
Challenge 1

1. a) simple language   ✓
    b) long sentences   ✗
    c) exciting pictures   ✓
    d) simple story structure   ✓
    e) chapters   ✗
    f) lots of characters   ✗
    g) exciting story plot   ✓

Challenge 2
1. a) letter; information
   b) advert; persuasion

Challenge 3
1. a) young children; story
   b) adults; letter
   c) teenagers (also accept adults); story

Pages 72–73
Challenge 1
1. a)

Fiction	Non-fiction
story	advert
picture book	biography
comic	recount
	report
	explanation

Challenge 2
1. a) rhetorical questions ✓
   b) humour ✓
   c) long paragraphs ✗
   d) memorable slogan ✓
   e) numbered steps ✗
   f) tempting descriptions ✓
   g) quotes from customers ✓
   h) address in top right corner ✗
   i) special offers ✓
   j) prices ✓

Challenge 3
1. a) biography   b) report
   c) instructions   d) letter

Pages 74–75
Challenge 1
1. a) princess   b) pirate   c) mermaid

Challenge 2
1. a) farm / castle / village
      Henry VIII / jester / ladies / bishop
   b) manor house / farm / dusty streets
      Lady of the Manor / butler / street urchins

Challenge 3
1. a) beach   b) swimming pool   c) school
   d) park

Pages 76–77
Challenge 1
1. a) Hazel said, "Please can I come too?"
   b) "Do you believe me?" Phoebe asked.
   c) "Believe it or not," Tim said, "it's true!"
   d) "Stop," the teacher shouted. "You need
      to listen to me!"

Challenge 2
1. a) "It's my birthday today," said Mum.
   b) The teacher said, "Stop talking now."
   c) "I will see you later," said William.
   d) "I have to leave immediately,"
      said Oscar.

Challenge 3
1. "The sand," remarked Grace, "is very soft and
   warm on my feet."
   "I know," replied Sandjit. "It is lovely, isn't it?"
   "Shall we paddle in the sea?" asked Grace.
   "Sounds fun," replied Sandjit, "but do you
   think it will be as warm as the sand?"
   "I doubt it," answered Grace, "but we can
   always warm our feet on the sand again."
   "Let's go!" shouted Sandjit and Grace
   together.
   **(1 mark for each correctly punctuated line of
   dialogue.)**
2. Children's own answers. 1 mark for each line
   spoken and correctly punctuated.

Pages 78–79
Challenge 1
1. a) story opening   3
   b) story ending   6
   c) characters that will be in it   1 / 2
   d) the settings in the story   1 / 2
   e) the main event   5
   f) the build-up   4

Challenge 2
1. a) The wolf eats Granny and puts   3
      her clothes on.
   b) Little Red Riding Hood sets   1
      off to visit Granny.
   c) The wolf eats Little Red-Riding   5
      Hood and falls asleep.
   d) The wolf rattles every time he   8
      walks and can't eat any more people.
   e) Little Red Riding Hood meets a wolf 2
      and tells him where Granny lives.
   f) When Little Red Riding Hood arrives 4
      at Granny's house she is surprised
      by her appearance.
   g) The woodcutter finds the wolf   6
      asleep and cuts him open. Little Red
      Riding Hood and Granny pop out
      unharmed.
   h) Little Red Riding Hood puts   7
      stones in the wolf's tummy and
      sews him up.

Answers

Challenge 3

1.

Before Writing	During Writing	After Writing
A, C, D, I, N, O, P, R	B, E, G, K, M	F, H, J, L, Q

Pages 80–81
Challenge 1

1. a) He <u>was</u> going to the park.
   b) They play<u>ed</u> happily all day at the beach yesterday.
   c) It <u>has</u> / <u>had</u> only just happened.
   d) You <u>are</u> in big trouble now.
   e) I <u>am</u> going home now.

Challenge 2

1. It was a hostile <u>enviroment</u>. The trees had branches that whipped back and left <u>bruses</u> on their skin. Harry had agreed to <u>acompany</u> them on this trip but was regretting that decision now. He had to continue though, otherwise there would have been <u>dissasterous</u> consequences. He wondered if he could <u>pursade</u> them to go along a shorter route back to camp. He was <u>desprate</u> to get back quickly so that he could rest and recover.

   a) environment   b) bruises
   c) accompany   d) disastrous
   e) persuade   f) desperate

Challenge 3

1.
> It <u>were</u> Sports Day. All the children <u>was</u> sitting in <u>they're</u> classes in the shade. They <u>is</u> all very excited<u>?</u> The first three races <u>was</u> going to be for the youngest children. Mrs <u>smith</u> was using the microphone to <u>announced</u> the races. The parents were all watching and <u>weighting</u> in anticipation of seeing <u>there</u> children run. The atmosphere <u>were</u> intense.

It **was** Sports Day. All the children **were** sitting in **their** classes in the shade. They **were** all very excited**.** The first three races **were** going to be for the youngest children. Mrs **S**mith was using the microphone to **announce** the races. The parents were all watching and **waiting** in anticipation of seeing **their** children run. The atmosphere **was** intense.

Pages 82–85
Progress Test 3

1. a) story; entertain
   b) recount; information

2. a) questions ✓   b) humour ✗ / ✓
   c) written in columns ✓   d) diagrams ✓ / ✗
   e) numbered steps ✗   f) tempting descriptions ✗
   g) quotes ✓   h) address in top right corner ✗
   i) captions ✓   j) photo / picture related to writing ✓

3. a) playpark   b) school
4. a) "My phone has broken," wailed Hermione.
   b) "My rabbit is called Doris," announced Fatima.
   c) "I need to lie down!" Murray exclaimed.
5. a) It **was** time to go home.
   b) I **am not** / **I'm not** going to school today.
6. a) **mis**represent   b) **re**take
   c) **re**inforce   d) **mis**understood
   e) **sub**merge   f) **tele**phone
7. a) sens**ible**   b) provis**ion**
   c) defens**ible**   d) horr**ible**
   e) ten**sion**   f) decis**ion**
8. a) The wedding **guest** was very happy.
   b) The magician said the spell **aloud**.
   c) She was given a **compliment** about her appearance.
9. a) small / little   b) relaxed / still / calm
   c) quiet
10. Mum: (*whispering to Dad*) When is this performance going to end?
    Dad: (*waking up from short nap and whispering*) Eh? What? Oh… yes. It's good isn't it?
    Mum: (*laughing and whispering*) How would you know? You've been asleep.
    Dad: (*sheepishly and quietly*) Only for a few minutes… sorry. It is rather long though isn't it?
11. a) refer**ral**   b) prefer**ring**   c) terrib**ly**

Pages 86–87
Challenge 1

1. a) a postcard to a friend   I
   b) a letter of complaint   F
   c) a conversation between friends in a story   I
   d) a note from your mum to a teacher   F
   e) a note to a friend   I
   f) a report about an incident   F

Challenge 2

1. **One mark for each correct line of dialogue.**
   "Hello, how are you?" asked Glen.

"Hello Glen, I am doing very well," replied Sam.
"Would you like to play football later?" asked Glen.
"Yes please, that would be great! What time shall I come?" asked Sam.
"I will be there at six so come whenever you would like to," replied Glen.
"Great, see you there!"

Challenge 3
1. I think that <u>we</u> should not have to wear <u>our</u> coats at school if <u>we</u> do not want to. <u>We</u> know whether <u>we</u> are cold so no one can tell <u>us</u> how <u>we</u> are feeling. <u>Our</u> opinion should be taken into account, don't <u>you</u> think?
2. Children's own answers (up to 3 marks). Answers will vary, e.g.
   It is suggested that students attending the school choose whether to wear coats outside. Some might argue that students are the best ones to decide whether the weather is too cold or not. Others feel that if the rule is not upheld, then many will not wear coats and will subsequently become ill.

Pages 88–89
Challenge 1
1. a) They <u>lived</u> in the house last year. past tense
   b) She <u>is walking</u> to school. present tense
   c) The lion <u>is roaring</u> loudly. present tense
   d) Next week, we <u>will bring</u> our toys to school. future tense
   e) I <u>went</u> to the cinema last night. past tense
   f) I <u>will write</u> the letter tomorrow. future tense

Challenge 2
1. a) The teacher **was** planning to give us a test.
   b) I watched carefully and **wondered** what the magician was going to pull from his hat.
   c) The animals **have** lots of places to sit in the shade.
   d) The Queen **was opening** the new building when she fell over.
   e) The cinema **is** open today.
   f) The computer **worked** yesterday.
2. a) They **helped** to bake the cakes for the sale.
   b) The children **made** a mess.
   c) The school **is** closed today because of snow.
   d) The parents **watched** the school play yesterday.

Challenge 3
1. a) We <u>could</u> go swimming today.
   b) The children <u>mustn't</u> go onto the grass.
   c) We <u>must</u> eat healthy food.
   d) The teacher agreed that they <u>could</u> go on the climbing frame.
   e) I <u>can</u> do anything I choose!
2. Answers will vary, e.g.
   a) It is snowing so we **must** wear our coats outside.
   b) The computer was broken so they **couldn't** use it.
   c) We **can't** eat lunch as the food is not ready.
   d) She asked if she **could** go to the toilet.
   e) We **shall** go out to play as the sun is shining.

Pages 90–91
Challenge 1
1.

When	Where	How
yesterday	everywhere	kindly
tomorrow	here	slowly
today	nearby	cheerfully
later	outside	urgently
now	there	quietly
often		

Challenge 2
1. I walked <u>quickly</u> to the shop as it <u>often</u> closed at lunchtime. I had been caught out <u>yesterday</u> as it was closed when I arrived. <u>Luckily</u>, it was open <u>today</u> and I bought my shopping. I <u>happily</u> waved goodbye to the shopkeeper and strolled <u>lazily</u> home.

Challenge 3
1. a) badly b) more
   c) least d) earliest
2. a) Getting things right is **more** important than finishing first.
   b) Our team played **badly** in the rain today.
   c) He was the **earliest** one to arrive.
   d) My favourite story is the one we have read the **least**.
3. Answers will vary.

Pages 92–93
Challenge 1
1. a) <u>The young man</u> walked to school.
   b) <u>An old lady with a stick</u> chased the dog away.
   c) <u>Yellow meadow butterflies</u> need to be protected.
   d) I walked towards <u>the sandy beach</u>.
   e) He was wearing <u>a nice blue shirt</u>.
   f) <u>The swimming pool in town</u> is new.

Answers

Challenge 2

1.

The happy dog	– ran away with the sausages.
A thoughtful girl	– worked hard at her maths.
My amazing friend	– always looks after me.
The cheeky monkeys	– chattered happily as they ate bananas.
The hungry child	– ran quickly home for tea.
The magical story	– took the children on an adventure.

2. Answers will vary.

Challenge 3

1. Answers will vary, e.g.
   a) The helpful man
   b) The angry swarm of bees
   c) My new car
   d) The useless bicycle
2. a) **The angry swarm of bees** chased after and stung the herd of antelope.
   b) I went to the tip and threw away **the useless bicycle**.
   c) I was scratched by **the unfriendly cat**.
   d) **The helpful man** helped the old lady onto the bus.
   e) I was excited to drive away in **my new car**.

Pages 94–95

Challenge 1

1. a) The car **over**took the lorry on the motorway.
   b) They had to **re**turn the items to the shop.
   c) He had not drunk enough so he was **de**hydrated.
   d) They had **mis**laid the remote control.
   e) The explorers were able to **dis**cover a new island.

2.
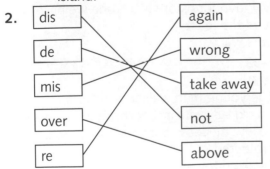

Challenge 2

1. Answers will vary, e.g.

dis-	mis-	over-	re-
disown	mistake	overturn	reintroduce
disheartened	misfortune	overcome	reissue

Challenge 3

1. a) I had to **re**do my work because it was incorrect.
   b) The robot was able to **de**fuse the bomb.
   c) The phone was **dis**connected from the socket.
   d) The boy **over**reacted to the football tackle.
   e) They had to **re**call the chocolate as it had been made wrongly.
   f) The children were **dis**appointed that sports day was cancelled.
   g) Sam **mis**understood the instruction.
2. Boris <u>was</u> a very **disobedient** boy and often **misbehaved**. People <u>would</u> **remark** on his bad behaviour. One day he <u>made</u> a big **mistake** as he <u>allowed</u> the bath he <u>was filling</u> to **overflow**; there <u>was</u> water everywhere!

Pages 96–97

Challenge 1

1. a) I **ran** home quickly.
   b) They **ate** their lunch slowly.
   c) The rabbits **are** unhappy.
   d) You **must eat** your vegetables!
   e) I **cried** during the film.

Challenge 2

1. a) Add the carrots to the pan. C
   b) How many carrots do I need? Q
   c) Carrots are good for you. S
   d) What a funny shape that is! E
   e) Why do I need to use carrots? Q
   f) Chop the carrots. C
   g) Do carrots help you see in the dark? Q
   h) I like eating carrots. S
   i) How strange carrot cake is! E
2. Answers will vary, e.g.
   a) I like playing football, do you?
   b) What a brilliant game football is!
   c) Football is my favourite thing to do.
   d) Play a game of football now.

Challenge 3

1. a) The cat is wet. ☐1
    b) I really like to eat lots ☐1
        of tasty vegetables.
    c) I walked home because ☐2
        it was dry.
    d) I ate lunch but I didn't ☐2
        have dessert.
    e) Cats do not like the rain. ☐1
    f) Fish like water, but ☐2
        cats do not like water.

2. a) Lizzie went to Freya's house **and** played
        games with her.
    b) Chan likes rugby **but** Jennifer prefers tennis.
    c) Coby was upset **as** he had lost his rabbit.
    d) **Unless** you work hard you will not improve.
    e) **However** much you cry, you will still not
        have any sweets!

Pages 98–99
Challenge 1

1. a) This is the table **that** everyone is admiring.
    b) I have a cat **whose** hair keeps falling out.
    c) Rosie is happy now **that** her skipping rope
        has been found.
    d) James, **whom** I think is funny, is my friend.
    e) The laptop, **that** I was using at the time,
        broke.
    f) The bike **which** I ride is very new.

Challenge 2

1. a) A magician is a person **who** performs
        magic tricks.
    b) I have two choices and I don't know
        which to choose.
    c) Children **who** misbehave are told off.
    d) I want to know **who** the child was that I
        spoke to.
    e) Jam, **which** is very sticky, is also very tasty.
    f) This is the book **that** everyone is rushing
        to buy.
    g) The activity centre **that / which** they are
        going to is overseas.

Challenge 3

1. a) I need someone **who** can look after my
        rabbits.
    b) I will take you to a shop **which** sells
        amazing sweets.
    c) Where did you buy the necklace **that** you
        wore last week?
    d) I have a brother **who** is exceptional at
        tennis.

e) His mum, **whom** he saw yesterday, gave
    him a huge hug.
f) I have a friend **whose** jewellery is very
    beautiful.
g) **Whichever** choice you make, you will
    upset someone!
h) Granny knits cardigans **which** are always
    beautiful.
i) We don't know the boy **who** fell out of
    the tree.

Pages 100–101
Challenge 1

1. a) The monkey fell off the ☐P
        branch.
    b) The boys will play football. ☐F
    c) The driver will have an accident. ☐F
    d) Sam injured his leg last week. ☐P
    e) The children completed ☐P
        the challenge.
    f) The swimmer is going ☐F
        to compete in a race.

Challenge 2

1. a) We **had** to work hard to finish the test
        yesterday.
    b) They **ran** very fast in last week's race.
    c) Chris **ate** his lunch very fast so he could
        play football.
    d) The giraffe will **come** out of his house
        soon.
    e) The playground **is** open today.
    f) When **will** the sun come out?
    g) He **has** worked hard to win that medal.
    h) The museum **was** interesting when they
        visited it.
    i) She **wanted** everyone to **come** to her
        party.

Challenge 3

1. a) was   b) are   c) is
    d) were   e) were   f) are
2. a) I **was** very late to school yesterday.
    b) It **is** now time to leave.
    c) They **were** in a lot of trouble last week.
    d) She **is** walking very fast along the road
        ahead of us.
    e) I **am** learning to ride my bike today.
    f) We **were** excited to see land ahead.

Pages 102–103
Challenge 1

1. a) She drove the car <u>as fast as possible</u>.
    b) The carpenter hit the nail <u>with a hammer</u>.

Answers

c) <u>As quickly as possible</u>, I sold the strange beads.

d) The aeroplane flew <u>swiftly through the cloud</u>.

e) The children walked <u>in silence</u>.

f) The adventurers set off <u>over the mountain</u>.

g) I went to watch the football <u>later than planned</u>.

h) The wolves were howling <u>loudly nearby</u>.

i) <u>Firstly,</u> I want to thank your parents.

Challenge 2

1. a) later that night — T
   b) finally — N
   c) near the woods — P
   d) over in the trees — P
   e) early that morning — T
   f) after the games — T
   g) out of the building — P
   h) secondly — N

Challenge 3

1. a) <u>Finally</u>, the duck eggs arrived. ✓
   b) <u>Later that morning,</u> we all had a snack. ✓
   c) The parents were all waiting <u>nearby</u> to meet us.
   d) <u>Early last week</u>, we left for our school trip. ✓
   e) My friend turned <u>down the nearest road</u>.
   f) Ariel and the Prince had to kiss <u>before sunset</u>.
   g) <u>Whenever it is possible</u>, I say thank you to my mum. ✓
   h) I saw lots of sweets <u>in the window of the shop</u>.
   i) <u>With a great deal of thought</u>, he made his choice. ✓

2. a) when   b) when   c) where
   d) when   e) where   f) when
   g) when   h) where   i) how

Pages 104–105
Challenge 1

1. a) The kit list said I needed shorts, t-shirts, shoes, socks, pants and a warm jumper.
   b) At school today, I have Maths, English, Science, Geography and PE.

Challenge 2

1. a) The girls, who were called Freya and Eliza, played in the playhouse.
   b) The chicken coop, which Harry's dad had built, had been at school for years.

c) The nursery children, who were all three or four years old, couldn't wait to go to the zoo.

Challenge 3

1. a) All day long, the children worked.
   b) Behind the pond, the frogs made their home.
   c) Under the sea, the mermaids sang their songs.

2. a)–c) Answers will vary, but each fronted adverbial must have a comma after it (1 mark for the fronted adverbial and 1 mark for the comma in each question).

Pages 106–107
Challenge 1

1. a) I have lots of hobbies (karate, reading, fishing and playing football) that I spend my free time doing.
   b) I had lots of presents for my birthday (money, clothes and cinema vouchers).
   c) She answered the question (after a long pause) and got it correct. / She answered the question after a long pause (and got it correct).

Challenge 2

1. a) Last night, Jacob – a security guard – caught two men trying to break into the school.
   b) The car – that was travelling very slowly – held up all the traffic.

Challenge 3

1. a) Aisha (my best friend) came over to play. ✓
   b) Mrs Thompson (my piano teacher inspired me) so much. ✗
   c) The weather was lovely beautiful, actually so we went to the beach. ✗
   d) The children all from – Class 5 – did not do as they were told. ✗
   e) Samuel a, thoughtful boy, liked to sit quietly and think. ✗

2. Mrs Thompson (my piano teacher) inspired me so much.
   The weather was lovely – beautiful, actually – so we went to the beach.
   The children – all from Class 5 – did not do as they were told.
   Samuel, a thoughtful boy, liked to sit quietly and think.

Pages 108–111
Progress Test 4

1. a) newspaper report ✓
   c) letter of apology to your teacher ✓
2. a) She <u>ran</u> to school today. past tense
   b) He <u>will kick</u> the football. future tense
   c) They <u>talked</u> too much past tense
   yesterday.
   d) You <u>are</u> beautiful. present tense
3. a) You **are** going to learn your times tables.
   b) They **built** a whole block of flats last year.
   c) I **have** lots of clothes to sell.
4. a) They listened <u>carefully</u> to the music.
   b) I hit the ball <u>very</u> hard.
   c) <u>Last week</u>, I ran a marathon.
   d) They crept <u>quietly</u> through the tunnel.
5. a) <u>The green crocodile</u> ate his lunch.
   b) <u>The old armchair with a broken cover</u> was thrown on the tip.
   c) It was lovely to see <u>the beautiful wildlife</u>.
6. a) I had to **re**verse down the lane.
   b) The accusation **up**set her.
   c) I was **dis**tracted by the television.
7. a) It is raining **so** the children had to stay inside.
   b) My friend likes broccoli **but / and** I like carrots.
   c) Samuel was sad **as / because** he had lost his favourite toy.
   d) **Unless** you do revision you will not do well in the test.
8. a) How much do these cost? [Q]
   b) How strange that they are so expensive! [E]
   c) Money doesn't grow on trees. [S]
   d) Earn some more money. [C]
9. a) This is the car **that** everyone wants to drive.
   b) I have a friend **who** has got three dogs.
   c) I love my dress **which** is new.
10. a) I ate my lunch earlier. [P]
    b) They are going to the seaside tomorrow. [F]
    c) He will fall over if he carries on! [F]
    d) They got lost in the hills. [P]
11. a) They all ran <u>out of the building</u>.
    b) <u>After the game</u>, they all had tea.
    c) They saw an owl <u>in the trees</u>.
    d) I arrived <u>earlier than planned</u> to watch the game.
12. He went to the shops to buy bacon**,** eggs**,** bread**,** milk and beans.
13. There were lots of stalls at the fair (tombola, barbecue, slides, bric-a-brac, etc).
14. B ✓
15.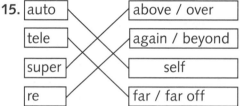

auto	above / over
tele	again / beyond
super	self
re	far / far off

16. a) Bats hang upside down. [F]
    b) Bats are scary. [O]
    c) Bats eat fruit. [F]
    d) Bats are not liked by humans. [O]
17. a) mourning = morning b) altar = alter
    c) stationery = stationary
18. "Come and line up," called the teacher.

Progress Test Charts

Progress Test I

Q	Topic	✓ or ✗	See pages
1	Root words		12–13
2	Root words		12–13
3	Prefixes		14–15
4	Suffixes		16–17
5	Prefixes		18–19
6	Adding prefixes and suffixes to root words		18–19
7	Homophones		20–21
8	Synonyms and antonyms		22–23
9	Synonyms and antonyms		22–23
10	Themes and conventions		28–29
11	Answering and asking questions		40–41

Progress Test 2

Q	Topic	✓ or ✗	See pages
1	Tricky spellings		64–65
2	Prefixes		50–51
3	Suffixes		52–53
4	Silent letters		54–55
5	Homophones		56–57
6	Confusing words		58–59
7	Using a dictionary		60–61
8	Using a thesaurus		62–63
9	Tricky spellings		64–65
10	Text types		24–25
11	Root words		12–13
12	Prefixes and suffixes to root words		18–19
13	Prefixes		50–51

Progress Test 3

Q	Topic	✓ or ✗	See pages
1	Audience and purpose		70–71
2	Different forms of writing		72–73
3	Characters and settings		74–75
4	Using dialogue		76–77
5	Editing		80–81
6	Prefixes		14–15
7	Suffixes		16–17 and 18–19
8	Homophones		20–21
9	Synonyms and antonyms		22–23
10	Playscripts		34–35
11	Suffixes		52–53

Progress Test 4

Q	Topic	✓ or ✗	See pages
1	Formal speech and writing		86–77
2	Different verbs		88–89
3	Different verbs		88–89
4	Adverbs		90–91
5	Noun phrases		92–93
6	Verb prefixes		94–95
7	Different sentences		96–97
8	Different sentences		96–97
9	Relative clauses		98–99
10	Tense choices		100–101
11	Adverbials of time, place and number		102–103
12	Commas for meaning		104–105
13	Brackets, dashes and commas		106–107
14	Brackets, dashes and commas		106–107
15	Prefixes		50–51
16	Facts and opinions		44–45
17	Homophones		20–21 56–57
18	Using dialogue		76–77

What am I doing well in? _____

_____

_____

_____

What do I need to improve? _____

_____